GUIDE TO
QUILTED
APPLIQUÉ

GUIDE TO QUILTED APPLIQUÉ

V A L   F R E E M A N

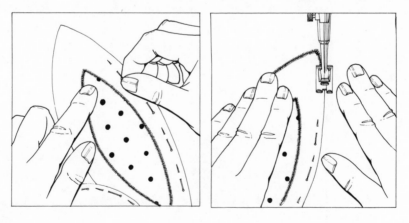

Sterling Publishing Co., Inc.   New York

Published in 1987 by
Sterling Publishing Co., Inc.
Two Park Avenue
New York, N.Y. 10016

ISBN 0–8069–6448–0 Trade
ISBN 0–8069–6450–2 Paper

Published by arrangement with Argus Books Limited.
This edition available in the United States, Canada and the Philippine
Islands only.

Phototypesetting by En to En, Tunbridge Wells, United Kingdom
Printed in U.S.A.

DEDICATION

To my parents, Anne and Harry Harrison, and to the parents of future generations of artistic children, who, like my parents, will encourage their offspring from an early age to know the joys of creativity with a needle and thread.

Closing their eyes to the scraps of cotton everywhere and opening their eyes with realization that their children are living in a world where a contented mind and body comes from the complete satisfaction of creating for themselves.

CONTENTS

PREFACE

The craft of appliqué is a joy, free from restrictions of the more formal pieced patchwork; the application of one fabric onto another (which is what the word appliqué means) leaves the needlewoman free to create more natural forms. When quilted, the final result is a sensual art form in fabric. To design your own work, instead of reproducing existing patterns is well within the capabilities of everyone, even beginners to the craft.

This little book guides you through all aspects of hand and machine work, enabling you to gain confidence. Starting with small projects, using your new skills you will be able to work up to the larger ones with ease.

It aims to elevate the once considered 'piecemeal hobby of patchwork' to the dizzy heights of designer quilts, giving 'no-nonsense' tips which eliminate unnecessary time wasting methods. Enjoy your fabric creativity, see easily achieved results, have fun and share your 'quilting fever' which is not only contagious, but also the most wonderfully rewarding, satisfying and useful of crafts for all ages and abilities.

I have written this book because I love my own work, I love sharing it with others and hopefully you will too, have fun.

ACKNOWLEDGEMENTS

To 'South View', Beckwithshaw, where I found the inspiration to make my first quilt.

To the North Euston Hotel, Fleetwood, where I wrote the first chapter.

To Bridge Syke, Elterwater, where I found the peace to write the rest.

To 'White Lodge', Harrogate, where I drew the illustrations in the beautiful garden.

To Mary Roberts who painstakingly typed the manuscript.

To Beverley Naylor for her artistic photography.

To Trevor Lockwood who suggested I made more of my work.

To Lynette Fogden and Sue Sharp who asked me to write my first article for 'Popular Crafts', which in turn led to this book and to Ann who helped me back the last quilt on time, and last, but by no means least my husband Graham, and our children Gail, Jonathan and James, who have, collectively over twenty-five years, helped and inspired me, through all our joint activities and parties, to create complete individuality around us, while tolerating a certain amount of inconvenience, before the longed for results were realized, but never complaining. My grateful thanks and love to you all.

INTRODUCTION

QUESTIONS ANSWERED

Starting out on the craft of appliqué requires guidance; this book should not only inspire you, but also help to give you all the short cuts to success with even your first project. There are many ways of achieving perfect results, some time consuming and other speedier methods, all of which have been tried and tested and the workable ones included throughout.

What is Appliqué? Appliqué is the ancient art form of applying one fabric on top of another. Its possible origin was probably out of necessity, ie. patching over a hole or tear. What seemed a practical solution at the time soon developed into a way of adding interest and individuality to personal belongings. We see it today in the form of numbers on football shirts — could this have derived from the crosses on the tunics of Crusaders? Countries are easily recognized by appliqué work on flags and banners. Instead of time consuming needlework it is useful in filling larger areas. Look around you in the shops, churches, museums, on clothing and quickly you develop a sixth sense for noticing appliqué work, be it from the ancient world or the modern. When you see it in your home every day you will feel proud to have learned a skill which has been passed down through the centuries.

Why Appliqué and not Patchwork? You can be freer with your design than with the geometric shapes of patchwork, while not struggling to match angles perfectly and cut on the cross diagonals. You will also be challenged by curves which capture nature in all its flowing, natural forms.

Why Quilted Appliqué? When the applied fabrics are quilted and a raised 3D effect is given to the work, this is not only sensual to the touch but pleasing to the eye, while, when used on bedquilts and clothing, provides extra warmth and comfort. This of course was the original necessity again of quilting three layers together: the decorative top layer and a lining, and sandwiched between them the old blanket in far off days, then cotton in its raw state, then wool, and as we have it today, batting in the form of man-made polyester wadding.

How do you do it? The basic principle, in a nutshell, is to sew one piece of fabric on to the top of another as neatly as possible, press it, lay it on top of a piece of batting (wadding), lay the two on top of a further layer of lightweight fabric, and quilt through all three with small neat running stitches.

How will this book help me? As with many other crafts, there are basic techniques, more advanced techniques, laborious and time saving techniques. This book will assist you in them all and show you the quickest methods to help you make an attractive project, be it a place mat or bedspread, that won't take you years to complete.

While there are many books on embroidery, a great deal on patchwork, not quite so many on appliqué, there are even fewer on the machine method — in particular appliqué and quilting done simultaneously by machine.

Why machine?   In my own case it was necessity again, like the earlier needlewoman. After years of having a needle in my hand, actually from the age of three, scarcely a day has gone by without my having stitched something, from silk pictures to making clothes. Suddenly I had arthritis in my thumb joints (and not from inactivity!). This was a scare and a challenge — what if they went before the brain? I just had to get my ideas down as soon as possible, panic set in and designs were flying through my head far faster than my hands could cope. I didn't want to spend the rest of my life wondering if I could have appliquéd such and such by hand. I now knew I just had to bury my old hang-ups of the man-made age and get a picture quilt through that machine while I was in the mood. I warn you now, it is a disease worse than immobilized thumb joints; by the end of this book I hope you have caught **'quilt fever'** in all its many forms and that it lives with you for the rest of your satisfying life!

Is the machine work quicker and not as attractive?   If worked with care and precision machine appliqué can have a 'definite' edge on hand work — the outline you put round your shapes sets off the motifs in a way hand work cannot. More about that later. The decorative finish of machine appliqué is often more pronounced than its hand worked sister.

Why not try both methods?   Do! You will then be your own judge of which method you actually prefer for each selected piece. Place mats, for every day wash and wear can be done by machine, and the large heirloom quilt, with many satisfying hours of quilting in it, can be done lovingly by hand.

When your quilting is over, you will feel a part of your soul has gone into one of the most relaxing and soothing of hobbies (even when you prick your finger — do remember this!). Paintings, sculpture, engraving, flower arrangements etc. are all admired and give inner pleasure to the viewer and its creators, but if you stand back at a quilt show, you will immediately notice how everyone wants to touch the work on view — even the men! For the quilter, the satisfaction is even greater, not only has she produced a thing of beauty, in her own eyes at least, but has also achieved putting it all together, which, unlike housework, cannot be undone!

Approach your work with a sense of humor, love and a desire to cherish every stitch, and you will not only delight yourself in the process, but create and give a little of your inner self expression and warmth to future generations, for their comfort and pleasure.

You will notice that the requirements are listed twice — once explanatory and once as a quick guide.

REQUIREMENTS AND REASONS FOR CHOOSING THEM

I am now going to answer questions on what to use and why we use it. At the end you will find a condensed list of requirements, for quicker reference.

Fabric Preferably 100% cotton. Lots of it with patterns, the smaller the better and plains from dark to light. The more you have of these in your collection the better. When just starting to collect don't go mad and buy up every small piece of cotton you find in the jumble pile on remnant day. Think about the texture and always try and aim at the same 'feel' to the fabric. Choose a color, fix it in your mind and search out all you can find with this color in it somewhere, however small the amount, i.e. I chose red, by this I mean red — not wine, maroon, plum, pink or orange — but red. From this small nucleus I can now pull out as many as two hundred small prints which readily co-ordinate. However, for your first project it will be sufficient to have two plains and three prints. Example:

Plain White.

Print White background with small blue flowers.

Plain Blue.

Print Blue with small white flowers with possibly a little pink in it.

Print Pink background with a mixture of blue and white in it. The shades of pink and blue should either exactly match each other or be the same tone in a shade darker or lighter.

   Once you have used a combination like this you will soon become accustomed to mixing the prints and plains, darks and lights and obtaining a correct balance.

Why cotton? Simply because it is the best fabric for the job you are doing, the easiest fabric to handle and in the long run, ensures even wear. To use a mixture of poly/cotton and 100% cotton pieces would cause uneven wear over a long period of time as a result of the manufactured fibre rubbing into the purer natural cotton. When a hand quilted article is washed, cotton sends out little crinkles (I refer to them as 'Crimples' named after the river which flows through the field at the back of our home) running across the surface from one row of stitches to the next. This gives a rippled effect and the quilt takes on a character all of its own. Poly/cotton bounces back without the 'crimples' and always retains a man-made look which is rather artificial. Poly/cotton also has a habit of being more transparent so that the seam allowances show through, especially on white and cream backgrounds. While not wishing to contradict myself, or confuse you, poly/cotton does have its uses, for example, backing a child's quilt, if the owner is likely to suck the edges, or screw it up in that enchanting way they have! Place mats and mixer covers etc. which, let's face it, will spend half their life in the washing machine, are also worthwhile backing in poly/cotton. Notice I only say 'backing' — there is still no substitute for cotton on the surface design. Sometimes you will need to use other fabrics, especially on picture quilts to create special effects: silks — ideal for ice, satins — ideal for water, voile — ideal for clouds, net — ideal for trees and also waves, corduroy — ideal for tree trunks (and little boys trouser patches! — yes, that's appliqué too). I am sure you will find many more for your picture quilts, but please remember the best discipline of all, when making a full size bed quilt, is to stick to cotton. Of course, the very best for this are the American craft cottons which are made especially for the purpose. As with most rules, there are some which are made to be broken but beware before venturing forth with tonal effects using cords, velvets, metallics, seersuckers, satins etc. Practice is needed in controlling the edges because these fabrics fray more easily and as I said earlier they are not suitable for constant washing, therefore only use them for wall hangings and picture quilts.

Sad to say for the declining British textile industry, the fine cottons with suitable small prints are no longer made in the quantities that they used to be. The patterns on them are more suited to the fashion trade than to soft furnishings. To use soft furnishing cotton, however appealing the patterns may appear, is to give your work a hard unyielding look. The beautiful puffiness of the hand quilting is lost in its general bulkiness and it is very hard on the fingers too. When sewing by hand and with machine appliqué the outlines will be more noticeable, possibly giving you trouble with ragged edges due to the coarseness of the weave. Cotton lawn, while having the correct patterns, is flimsy and wears too easily and its weight and texture is too fine for continual wear. Again as with poly/cotton, the seam allowances are difficult to disguise in the paler shades.

Perhaps, before long, Britain will again weave and print fine cottons with we quilters in mind, but until that day arrives, better to use the tried and tested American craft cottons.

What is Batting?   Batting, wadding, stuffing — they all mean exactly the same. Now that that's cleared up you'll want to know which kind to use — there is no mystery, it's all in the thickness.

What type of batting/wadding?   The most used and easily available at present is polyester/batting/wadding. It is manufactured in many thicknesses and classified in weight per square yard or per square metre, as follows:

2 oz. per square yard. 67 grams per square metre — This is the thinnest and suitable for place mats and beginners.

4 oz. per square yard. 135 grams per square metre — Ideal for soft sculpture, larger projects, cushions, quilt blocks, hand quilting baby quilts and the more experienced quilter.

6 oz. per square yard. 202 grams per square metre — Just perfect for machine work, though care should be taken when first putting under the machine foot.

8 oz. per square yard. 270 grams per square metre — For the expert, but be warned that it is not only very thick to handle, on or off the machine, but also very HOT to have around you and very heavy on the bed! However, the height is superb and the shadows deep and rich. Though should you attempt to hand work it your stitches will have to be much larger than with the thinner batting.

When choosing your batting make sure you get one with a sprayed finish for picture quilts and machine work; the surface will be smooth and will help you tremendously. The unsprayed fluffier looking variety is ideal for hand quilting, providing it is of good quality and of an even thickness. Test this by lifting a section and viewing the light through it. Don't confuse this with 'stuffing' or 'filling' used in soft toys and padded appliqué. An old wool blanket can still be used with good effect, as in the olden days, but check it has quite even wear — you don't want a hole or thinner bit in the middle. Wash it and dry it on a good windy day to bounce out the fibres; do not have it dry cleaned, as this will give a very hard, harsh feel and make it difficult to quilt through.

What kind of thread?   Use the old fashioned kind — 100 per cent mercerized cotton thread is better as it doesn't cut through the surface of the cotton appliqué motifs. Poly thread does, it is also thinner and does not give the same raised satin stitch outline when you are machine stitching. With hand stitching I find it is annoying on the hands. Use quilting thread for hand quilting and it is a good idea to wax the thread for hand sewing. You will also need a large spool of inexpensive tacking thread.

What is the best backing fabric?   Again, a matter of situation dictates the answer more than what is 'correct'. The 'correct' choice is really up to you. Poly/cotton really doesn't enter into it; your quilt will have an artificial look, unloved and unlived in, but the main reason for choosing cotton is simply HEAT. If you are making a quilt for a bed you do so to keep you warm. Poly/batting/wadding only retains its heat when sandwiched between two layers of pure 100% cotton but does not when encased between two layers of a manufactured fibre or synthetic fabric. Cotton backing also prevents the quilt from running off the bed in the night!

Having machine appliquéd and quilted a king size quilt it is a good idea to try and get the backing in one piece. Sometimes this is only available in sheeting, which nowadays seems to be mainly a mixture of fibres. Also a quilt made by this method is not quilted through the backing like a hand worked piece through three layers, so the backing fabric will have to stand up to rubbing from the polyester batting. This is a case when a mixed fibre king size sheet is ideal as long as the largest percentage is still cotton. It will be crease resistant and will not need ironing. Quilts should never be ironed after they have been hand or machine quilted or washed; the heat from the iron will completely destroy the filling and flatten it.

Needles   No. 7: Crewel for hand quilting, No. 8: Betweens for hand quilting. The choice is up to you, whichever you feel happiest with. I like either of these but remember, you will have it in your fingers a long time so best be comfortable to begin with.
No. 5 — 10: Sharps for the hand embroidered details and hand appliqué.

Thimbles   Here again I prefer the leather finger guards to the more conventional metal ones — unless, of course, someone gives you a real gold or silver one! The leather ones have a metal tip to them and also allow the finger tip to breathe.

Pins   Long stainless steel — they may be in there a long time and if for any reason the atmosphere is a little damp they could rust, so don't use the ones from the office desk. Don't use the glass headed kind for machine appliqué as sometimes you will find it necessary to ride the machine foot over the head of the pin.

Beeswax   in a holder.

Soft to medium pencil.

Water erasable pencil   Mixed feelings about this; the chemical reaction on the fabric has not yet stood the test of time to know whether it will rot the fabric in a decade or so. This is best kept for use with beginner projects and the pencil for the heirloom quilts. This leads me into mentioning my own invention 'The Patch Stamp' which is used with a washable ink and the same could be said about it as the water erasable pen. However, I wash mine out after sewing the patches together and before quilting or making up, so the ink is not left in the fabric. 'The Patch Stamp' idea came to me having just watched a class of small children trying desperately to draw an accurate template, cut it, then draw round it just as accurately, not to mention sewing as perfectly on the line, and all in one lesson. It was no wonder there was disappointment on their little faces, going home from their first needlework class with nothing to show Mom and Dad but a misshapen piece of cardboard!

So 'the Patch Stamp' was born; I simply reversed the thinking on the cutting and seam allowance lines. Solid on the outside for cutting fabric, broken lines on the inside for hand stitching or machine stitch guidance, then stamp it down on the fabric, and hey presto, the pattern is precise and perfect, ready for stitching, and built into your own choice of fabric. The dotted line can also be used to cut templates if a traditional method of patchwork is followed.

¼ inch (6 mm) strip of stiff cardboard × 6 inches (15 cms)

T square

Scissors   Long sharp dressmaker kind and short sharp to the point needlework ones.

Tracing Paper

Bonding Agent   Iron on, double sided fusible webbing.

Quilting Hoop   Or floor frame for a large quilt. If space doesn't permit you can actually do the quilting on your knee (known as lap quilting).

Powdered Starch   For when the going gets too hot, rub a little on your hands to keep them dry, it also helps the thread to stay clean and not leave dirty marks on your work.

Cutting out table   If you do not have a large table perhaps you will find this idea worthwhile investing in. You can always share it with the DIY member of the household, unless that's you, then you have a double reason for buying it. It is better to buy two decorating tables from the DIY store (while you are in there pick up a metre stick or a yardstick — also). Erect the two tables side by side, this gives you a space at workable height of 6 × 4 feet (1.85 m × 70 cms). They are quickly erected side by side, are just as easily collapsed and put away to store neatly and they even have a carrying handle. They are better still when covered with an old blanket or mattress pad, or perhaps you could run to a commercially quilted fabric, cut it slightly larger than the tables, cut off the four corners diagonally and stitch a short length of elastic round them as on a fitted bottom sheet. This will keep the cloth a snug fit and gives a non-slip surface to work on and to pin to. An easy way to fit the corners (and flat sheets on the bed) is to tie a knot at each corner, pull slightly inwards and backwards underneath the worktop (mattress) making a flat sheet into a fitted one instantly. If you plan to do a lot of sewing you will find this is invaluable and a worthwhile investment, particularly if you are short of space.

Iron   With an extension cord so you can press on the table without disturbing the layout.

Worktable   When you are machine quilting larger projects, another 'must' I'm afraid is the largest worksurface possible, for the heavy fabric to sit on rather than it pulling off the edge of a smaller table. The decorator tables already mentioned are too fragile for the weight of the machine. Here again, if the dining table is too precious, the kitchen table too small and storage at a premium, try buying a door! A single hardboard door and two trestles, or just balance the door on top of a smaller table.

Sewing Machine   With a swing needle which is able to zig-zag for machine appliqué. If your machine slips use a wet cloth or similar underneath it. Last but not least patience and lots of it but it's free.

REQUIREMENTS — A QUICK REFERENCE LIST

TO CROSS REFER WITH NUMBERS AT THE BEGINNING OF EACH PROJECT

1 Cotton fabrics, prints and plains

2 Batting (wadding)
   2 ounces 67 grams
   4 ounces 135 grams
   6 ounces 202 grams
   8 ounces 270 grams

3 Calico or any fabric for backing

4 Mercerized sewing thread

5 Needles, Crewels, Betweens

6 Leather thimbles

7 Pins (long steel)

8 Quilting thread

9 Large spool household tacking thread

10 Beeswax in a holder

11 Medium soft pencil and dark pen

12 Strip of cardboard $\frac{1}{4}$ inch (6 mm) $\times$ 6 inch (15 cms), also pieces of cardboard, stiff paper and clear plastic

13 T square

14 Scissors— large cutting out dressmaker shears and small sharp pointed embroidery

15 Tracing paper and brown paper

16 Bonding Agent

17 Quilting hoop or frame

18 Powdered starch and spray starch

19 Cutting out table

20 Iron

21 Water erasable pencil and Patch Stamp

22 Sewing machine with a swing needle, capable of zig-zag stitch

ENLARGING PATTERN PIECES USING A GRID

Using a sharp pencil or fine point pen and a ruler, draw out a grid on a large piece of paper. The squares of the grid should have the measurement indicated on the pattern; in this book the patterns are transferred onto a finished size grid of 1 inch (2.5 cm).

When the grid is complete, copy the details from each square of the book pattern onto the paper grid, making sure all lines meet.

You now have full size pattern pieces— check the individual instructions for the project you are making to see if you need to add a seam allowance or whether this is already included.

Pre-ruled squared paper is also sold for dressmaking use. This can be used if the finished grid size is the same as the size that the pattern requires.

PREPARATION AND STORAGE

PREPARATION OF FABRICS

All the fabrics should be pre-washed in warm water to pre-shrink and test for color fastness, before cutting out. If you use a tumble drier it is a help to put a large bath towel in with them to stop them twisting together. Don't use a detergent with built in fabric softener as this will make them harder to finger press when you turn under the hem allowance.

I usually iron dry the smaller pieces and dry the larger ones on the line. When ironing, spray starch a little as you go; this not only gives them back their crispness, it also helps to stop any fraying when cutting out for machine work. Please don't treat this time as boring or not necessary. I know only too well the eagerness to get those scissors into that new pile of lovely, mouth-watering cloth. It is, however, absolutely vital to the finished product's washing and wearing ability in its future life. Also it is an ideal time to get to know your fabrics; while ironing them, get the 'feel' of the design and the way it looks its best. So often, having planned my work thoroughly, or so I thought, I found that on the ironing board it appealed to me in a different way.

Thread should be waxed before hand quilting for strength and to keep it tangle free. It is also a useful tip to thread up ten or more needles and have them by you ready for use, sometimes using two in different directions when quilting in a frame. I wax mine even when using quilting thread. For this, use a block of beeswax which is obtainable in a plastic holder with grooves; the thread runs through this as it protects your fingers from getting cut on the thread. The block never seems to run out, though occasionally you may find it useful to warm the wax and reshape it into a disc again.

Storing Never store in plastic. This will cause sweating, especially, if like me, you find the only large cupboard is next to a hot water pipe! Try to roll your quilts — ask at the local fabric shop for a left over hard cardboard roll. Roll them over this with an old sheet rolled in with it, or if space doesn't permit, fold and store inside an old pillow case. A word on folding, try to avoid the in half and in half again classic fold, which will produce the most strain on the most used part of the quilt. Instead try folding in thirds each way and always re-fold differently each time you put it away.

CHOICE
OF
COLOR

The choice of color for your project is entirely your own! If you see a tempting pattern, you immediately wish it was yours, liking it instantly the way it is. Why then make it in beiges and browns, when the way it is worked is in reds and yellows or pinks and greens? Perhaps initially you liked the pattern and then realized it did not match your room scheme, but after altering it you then decide it doesn't look quite so good as it did in its original format!

It lifted your day in its original form, so let's lift every day by copying the color exactly.

Of course, that is one option, the second option is to change just one of the fabrics to make it fit in with your scheme and to be just individually you.

It is a good idea to have a different color on each side of what you are making, one to match your room as it is at present, and one to be an exact copy of the work which originally inspired you. The chances are, before long, you'll be changing the room to fit the original choice!

As with all the methods described, try everything once, and for color use colored paper rather than run the risk of cutting up expensive fabrics. Glue them in their shapes to a stiff cardboard, sit back and see if you can live with it. If so, sew it. A general rule on interior design, is that if you go into a room and are instantly aware, for more than a week, that something is new in there, then you know for certain that it is wrong for the room. So, best to use the colored paper method!

The color you choose for a room can change the whole atmosphere you live in. Pale green has always been accepted as a safe shade, but don't forget to introduce a small amount of yellow to bring in instant sunshine; introduce coral and you warm a room, almost like sunset, it glows. Plan a room, a quilt or just a cushion to match a favorite piece of porcelain. Place the cushion on a chair next to the table with the porcelain on and just see the co-ordinated difference it brings. North facing rooms need warm colors, as south facing rooms need cooler tones but can look devastating in rainbow shades. Try not to be too conservative, your home should tell the world it is the happy place you live in. Entrance halls can be lively and very colorful, so imagine coming in on a wet, snowy, cold or foggy day to a warm bright sunny coloring of orangey yellow. You are not likely to dwell in the entrance for the whole day, so why not create an immediate glow from which you can comfortingly propel yourself to a more relaxed color scheme for sitting in the rest of the day.

Regarding actual fabric colors on quilts, try to balance the lights and darks — too many pastels end up looking wishy-washy, too many darks together look depressing and dismal. As discussed in fabric choice at the beginning, pick up one color and choose several small prints with the same shade or tone of color to link through the patches. Balance plains with prints; setting colors and motifs is rather like flower arranging, try to give each fabric space to be on its own, to breathe and be seen, at the same time relating to the other pieces and colors around it.

We are all different and our work must reflect that fact, so while this is only an outline guide I do hope you will try to create your own schemes for your work, while acknowledging the fact that if you really do see something out of this world, you will try to copy it in its original form. You never know, the stitcher of the original design possibly tried it in a thousand and one ways, including yours, before settling on the color which has just taken your eye!

HAND APPLIQUÉ

◁   *Cut out.*
_____ *Clip in a straight line almost to the seam line.*
– – – *Fold inwards first, or clip off if the fabric looks bulky.*

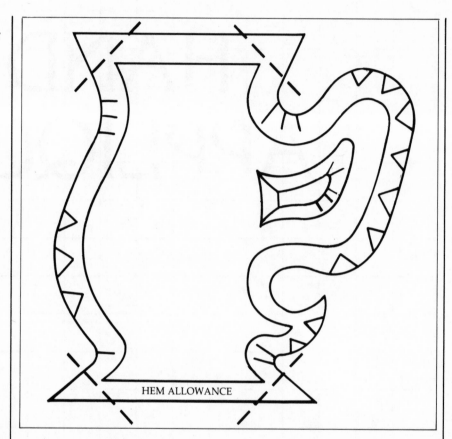

HEM ALLOWANCE

INTRODUCTION

This is a very complex diagram for reference only. It shows very clearly each type of snip, clip and nick you may encounter on outward and inward curves, including the treatment of corners. Take your time to study it carefully; if you are a first time stitcher and not used to the basic dressmaking techniques, it will save you hours later on. If you are a dressmaker, then lucky you, your appliqué work is going to be all sunshine from now on.

It is only necessary to snip the inside points, but you may notch the outside ones if you wish. Take care not to go right up to the seam line as this could cause a halt, or break, in the continuity of the curve and change the shape of a circle to a hexagon!

METHOD

REQUIREMENTS
1 4 5 6 7 9 11 12 14 15 16 19 20 21 optional

Trace off the selected design using the tracing paper, then trace off each motif separately. If a motif is repeated more than once on the final design then trace a separate pattern for each piece. Go over the outside of the overall tracing with a thicker line. When using a light colored background fabric, I have found it very useful to slide this under the fabric, so that the design shows through it — this acts as a placement guide.

Cut out the pattern shapes.

If using the pattern more than once cut a cardboard or plastic template for each piece. Lay the selected fabrics face down on to the work table. Place the cut out templates face down on top of them and draw round the outside edges carefully using the soft pencil — don't press too hard, you don't want it to show through. Using the strip of cardboard, place it alongside the pencil line and gradually move it around the shape, pencilling in a second, outer line ¼ inch (6 mm) away from the original line. This is the seam allowance which you will turn under.

Cut the motifs out carefully on the outside line, using short, sharp scissors

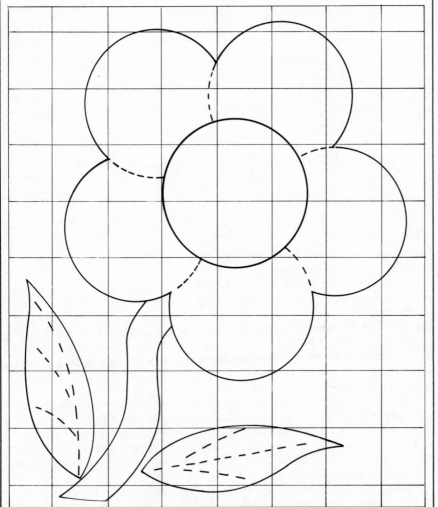

Flower. Full size after hem allowance is turned in. Trace each section separately, see diagram next page.

Each square = 1 inch (2.5 cm)

Traced Separate Motifs

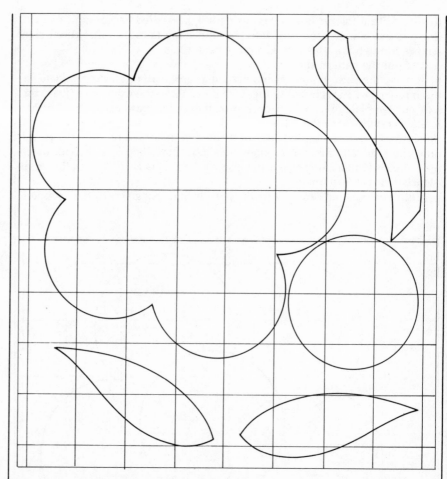

Each square = 1 inch (2.5 cm)

which are ideal on the curves and for snipping into the seam allowances.
Look closely at the first diagram.

Lay all the cut out fabric motifs down on to the work area, fold the seam
allowances towards you, on to the wrong side of the fabric. Press with a
warm iron. When doing curves you can either use a cardboard template in
the center of the fabric and fold the seam allowance down over this before
pressing, or use the traditional method, which is to run a little running stitch
in a contrasting thread on the seam line. Draw this up very slightly indeed
and the edge will curl over for you, enabling you to press with the iron on the
wrong side, before hemming into place.

Full circular shapes are rather tricky so it is best to cut a thin cardboard, or
thick paper template for each one. Place on the reverse of the fabric, run a
running stitch round the outside edge, this time halfway between the edge
and the seam line. Pull this up tightly, carefully take out the template, fasten
off with a backstitch and press. You now have a perfect circle for appliquéing
to the background.

Stems are not difficult. Iron a piece of bonding agent on to the reverse side
of the selected fabric and peel off the backing. Using your pattern, draw

round it on the reverse side. If this is a little tricky on the tacky surface, then use the water erasable pencil. Use the $\frac{1}{4}$ inch (6 mm) cardboard to mark in the seam allowance, cut out, then cut across the corners.

Fold over the edges on to the wrong side and carefully press with the very tip of the iron, taking care not to touch the center section of the stem, where the revealed bonding agent is visible — this would make the surface of the iron very sticky indeed. Only press the seam allowance down, you will now have a stem with mitred corners and firm to the touch, ready to hem in place. Should part of the stem be underneath a petal, do not turn this edge under, otherwise you will add general bulk. Ideally stems should be cut on the bias (cross grain) of the fabric. If you have sufficient, this makes them more pliable and easier to get a curved effect, but this is not necessary on primitive, or straight stemmed flowers.

Now you have pressed under all the seam allowances take up a basting thread, thread the needle and tie a knot at one end, keeping the knot on the top of the motif. Tack with smallish stitches round the edges of the shape, to hold down the seam allowance. By keeping the knot on the surface, you will be able to clip it off and remove the tacking threads when you hemstitch the

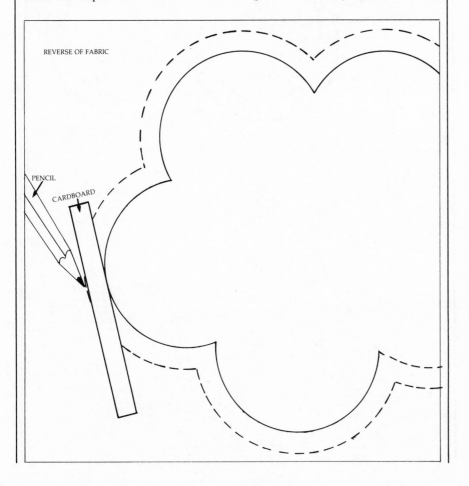

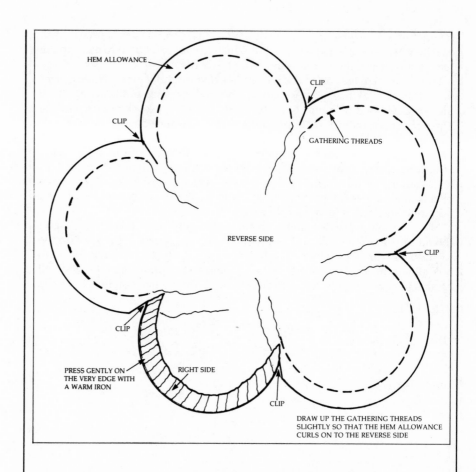

HEM ALLOWANCE

CLIP

CLIP

GATHERING THREADS

REVERSE SIDE

CLIP

CLIP

PRESS GENTLY ON
THE VERY EDGE WITH
A WARM IRON

RIGHT SIDE

CLIP

DRAW UP THE GATHERING THREADS
SLIGHTLY SO THAT THE HEM ALLOWANCE
CURLS ON TO THE REVERSE SIDE

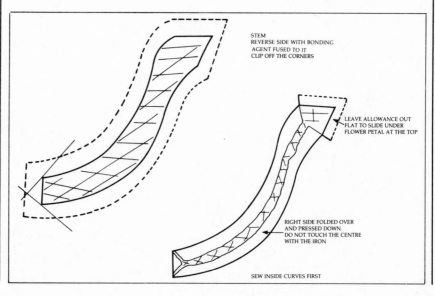

STEM
REVERSE SIDE WITH BONDING
AGENT FUSED TO IT
CLIP OFF THE CORNERS

LEAVE ALLOWANCE OUT
FLAT TO SLIDE UNDER
FLOWER PETAL AT THE TOP

RIGHT SIDE FOLDED OVER
AND PRESSED DOWN.
DO NOT TOUCH THE CENTRE
WITH THE IRON

SEW INSIDE CURVES FIRST

shapes in place. Press the basted pieces well, on both sides, taking care again not to touch that center section of the bonding agent.

Either use the placement guide as previously mentioned or carefully mark round the outline of the overall design, on to the background fabric, so that you can see where to place the motifs. When making a single item you may prefer to place 'by eye', but please pay great attention to detail when making exact copies, i.e. place mats, blocks for bedspreads or matching cushions, etc. Measure meticulously, in every way possible, before starting to hem down, you will be surprised how even the smallest misalignment can show up on the finished article.

You may like to use the water erasable pencil to mark the pattern position on the right side of the fabric. It is very useful when lining up special surface design and you need to keep an eye on the right side of the fabric at all times. My notes on this pen are in the hand quilting section, so if in doubt, read this first.

If you prefer not to tack the seam allowances under, you may prefer to roll the seam allowance between the finger and thumb, backwards on to the wrong side, hemming down with the tiniest stitches possible as you go (this is also referred to as blind stitching) — it doesn't mean you can't see to do it — - it just means you shouldn't see it when you have done it! With a tiny stitch on the top and a slightly larger one underneath, bringing the needle up through the background fabric and breaking the surface directly on the edge of the motif, the needle then passes through the edge of the motif. Take it back down through the background fabric, leave a slightly larger stitch underneath and come up to the top again.

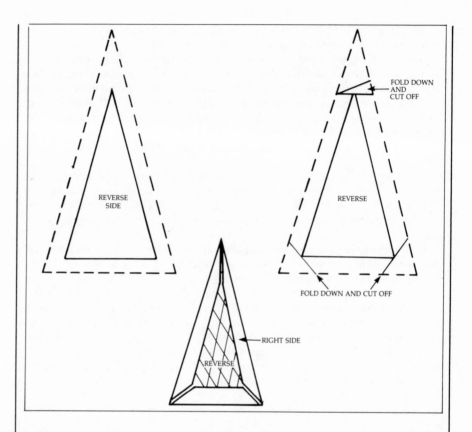

If you are rolling under the hem allowance, rather than tacking first, it can be difficult if you have a thumb and finger like mine. Don't then feel 'you can't' — just get a little pointed end cocktail stick, place it under the hem allowance, roll the fabric over this, away from you, and as you hem stitch the edge down, continue to slide the cocktail stick along the edge, turning the fabric against the firm stick as you go. You will be doing a rolling action with your fingers, rather than a pushing against nothing action — this is much easier when your grip starts to go a little.

When turning under a sharp point, refer to the diagrams. Fold the point down across the bottom of the point, on the seam allowance line, snip a little off it, fold the two outer edges over this, trim a little of them away until you are happy they don't show on the front, then hem stitch down in the usual way.

Press your finished work on the right side, then on the reverse. It is now ready to be quilted. This can be done by hand or machine, but having gone this far by hand your work is worth hand quilting and will look better for it.

Follow the directions in the Hand Quilting Chapter page 43.

MACHINE APPLIQUÉ

See Plate 7 in color section

INTRODUCTION

Machine Appliqué is hemless, as opposed to the turning under of a hem in hand appliqué. You actually sew over the raw-cut edge, equally with the background fabric, using a neat satin stitch setting on the zig-zag stitch of your sewing machine.

This has the distinct advantage of outlining the motifs in a more pronounced way than with hand stitching and the effect gives a hand drawn look to the work. Aiming for a perfect finish is every bit as important as with hand work; here too, patience is an asset. Select a pattern of your own choice, or use the Butterfly pattern here to try out machine appliqué.

METHOD

REQUIREMENTS
1 2 3 4 7 11 14 15 16 18 19 20 21 22

Main requirement is a sewing machine with a zig-zag stitch, commonly known as a swing needle. You will require an appliqué foot too. I never use one but when just beginning it does give you a clearer view, taking away any guess work.

Scissors with a very sharp point, and paper scissors so as not to blunt your best ones.

Trace off your chosen pattern using the tracing paper and dark pen. You do not need a seam allowance on machine work, so please remember, what you cut is what you sew — no room for even a slight error in the cutting out.

FABRIC REQUIREMENTS FOR A BUTTERFLY CUSHION

2×16 square inch cream plain
1×16 square inch 2 ounce batting
1×2¹/₂ yards × 5 inch for frill (print) border
1×12 square inch dark print for main wings
1× 7¹/₂×2 inch body
1×12×10 inch upper and lower wings pale print
1×12×4 inch upper and lower inner wings plain or medium print
14 inch zip fastener
1 yard bonding agent

I do emphasize that you always make a full size tracing even on a mirror image design. Because there are not full width patterns, place on a vertical line to be sure of exact repeat. Lay the tacky side of the bonding agent face down on to the reverse side of the traced paper. Use small pieces of decorator's masking tape to keep it in position if you have difficulty. You should be able to see the lines of the design through as you have used a dark pen, if not, go over the lines again with something thicker.

On the paper side of the bonding agent trace off the design again. Draw one outline for each separate motif, even when the motif is repeated several times — no short cuts here, one for each time it appears. Cut these shapes out of the bonding agent, using paper scissors.

Select your fabric and put the cut out traced shapes, tacky side down, on to the reverse side of the selected fabrics. When you are satisfied each shape is on its correct fabric and the top and bottom of the pattern as near as can be to the straight grain of the fabric, press down slightly with the iron. Cut round the paper shapes and peel off the paper backing. Your motifs are now ready for you to apply to the background material. Decide on this and cut accordingly.

If making a trial block for a full size quilt try a 15 inch (38 cms) cut at 16 inches (40.5 cms) to start with; sometimes appliqué can reduce the size of the background at first, so it is better that you leave some to trim off later. This applies very much when you are machining and quilting all in one go.

Lay the background fabric on the work table and slide the heavily traced outline of the pattern underneath it. You will be able to see the outline clearly

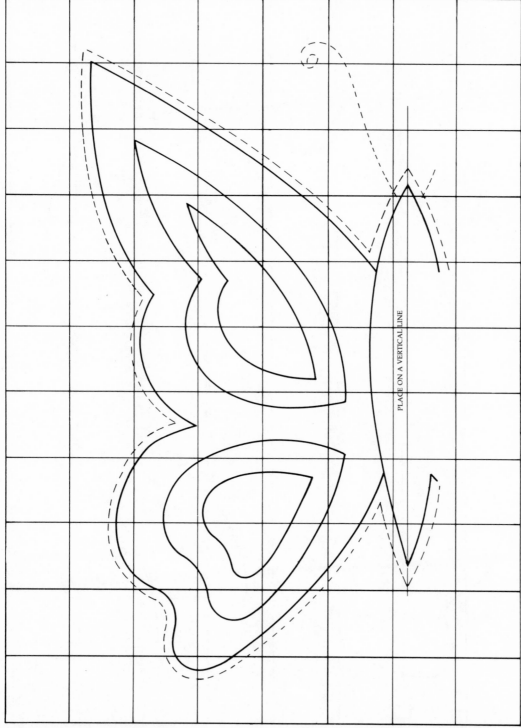

PLACE ON A VERTICAL LINE

Each square = 1½ inches (3.9 cm)   See Plate 12 in color section

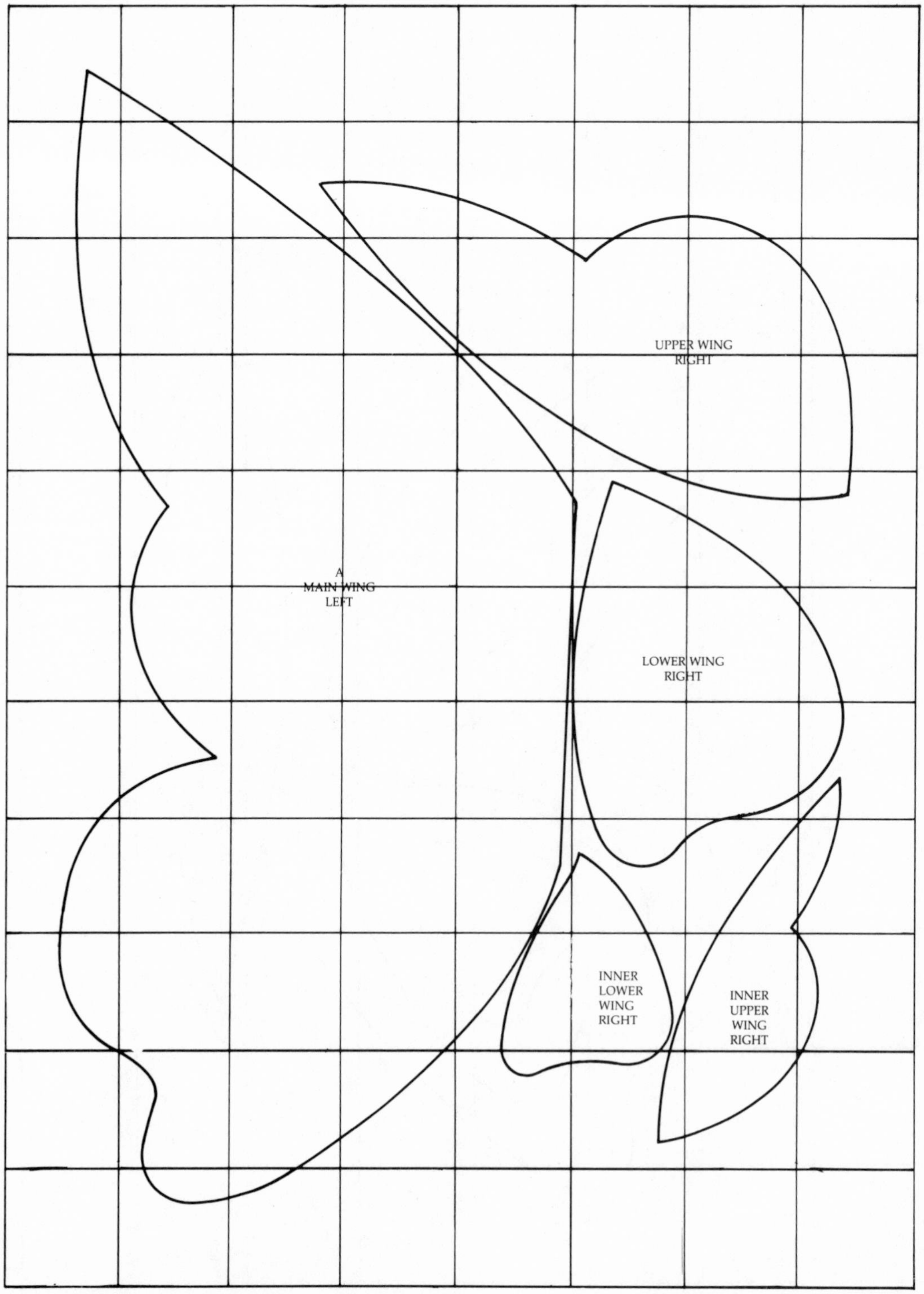

UPPER WING
RIGHT

A
MAIN WING
LEFT

LOWER WING
RIGHT

INNER
LOWER
WING
RIGHT

INNER
UPPER
WING
RIGHT

Each square = 1½ inches (3.9 cm)

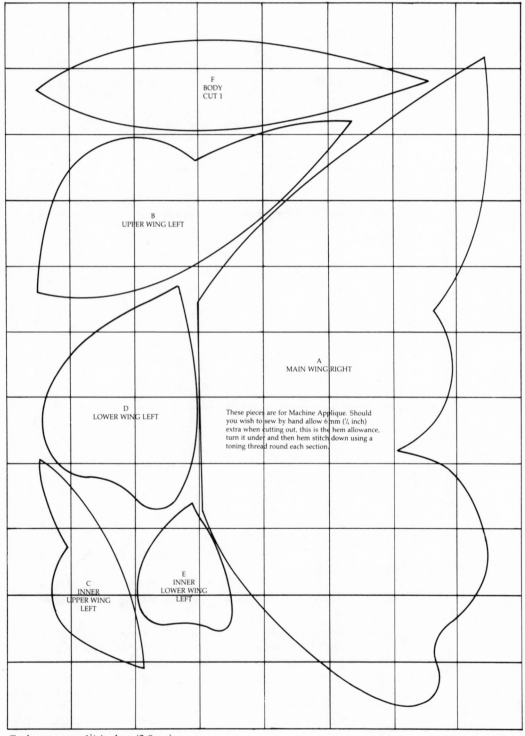

F
BODY
CUT 1

B
UPPER WING LEFT

A
MAIN WING RIGHT

D
LOWER WING LEFT

These pieces are for Machine Applique. Should you wish to sew by hand allow 6mm (¼ inch) extra when cutting out, this is the hem allowance, turn it under and then hem stitch down using a toning thread round each section.

C
INNER
UPPER WING
LEFT

E
INNER
LOWER WING
LEFT

Each square = 1½ inches (3.9cm)

through it if your background color is light and it will act as a placement guide for your shapes to follow.

Carefully place the bonded shapes down on to the background, right sides uppermost and when you are quite satisfied they are directly over the shadow, press down with the iron. If you are working on a composite picture quilt, do the pieces farthest away from you first, i.e. the outer wings of the butterfly before the inner, and lastly, the body; the sun in the sky before the clouds if it is peeping out from behind them, the horizon before the trees etc. They will now be bonded to the background for you to sew, avoiding any movement while you do so. Lightly mark with your soft pencil or water erasable pen the character lines on faces, veins on leaves, imitation folds, rays of the sun, etc. and you will now be able to see where they are when you come to machine over them.

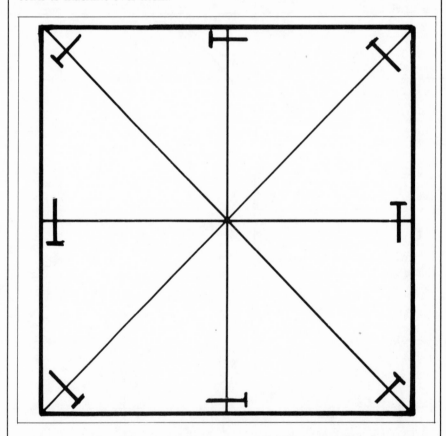

Folded square of fabric — lightly press with iron. Fold pattern in same way and match center point to line them up together. Matching the creases, pin on outside edges.

If you wish to center the design, do so by folding the background fabric in half and in half again and then diagonally, pressing with the iron to show the creases from side to side and corner to corner. If you fold the traced paper in the same way, the center point should then be lined up and match exactly.

If you choose a dark background fabric and cannot see the placement guide through, put it on top of the fabric and slide the motifs underneath until the design is lined up ready for pressing. Take great care when removing the

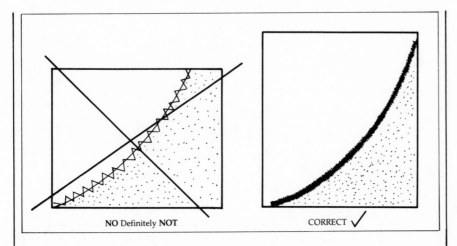

NO Definitely **NOT**   CORRECT ✓

tracing paper, so as not to disturb the loose pieces underneath. In fact you can try pinning the traced placement guide down at the outer corners and pressing slightly to fix the shapes before removing the tracing, then press again when you have.

Cut a large square of brown paper at least 3 inches (7.5 cms) larger on all sides than the background, place the block in the center and pin all the way round.

Using a fine needle on the machine, thread the top with a color thread of your choice. I always use a contrast with machine appliqué but if you prefer a toning thread to match the color of each shape, then that is up to you.

You may prefer to experiment later on but essentially at this stage you are learning how to work efficiently and neatly. Use white or cream underneath, it really doesn't matter, just make sure that the tension is set so that the bottom thread does not come through on to the top surface. Set the zig-zag stitch width at approximately $\frac{1}{8}$ inch (3mm) and shorten the stitch so the stitches are almost parallel to one another, as with a very neat buttonhole stitch. I am not going into the workings of the machine too much in detail, as I assume, if you already own one, you will have read the manual and already know how to operate it to achieve the various stitches it is capable of giving you. Always have a little practice first and study the diagrams on this page. The stitches themselves should equally cover the cut edge of the motif and the background fabric.

Start by stitching the underneath shapes first, as you did when pressing them down. A petal and a stalk before a sepal and a leaf, etc.

When you arrive at a sharp corner, stop the machine, raise the foot, leaving the needle in it in the down position. Pivot the fabric to the direction you wish it to go, lower the foot and continue sewing again.

Using the appliqué foot you will be able to see when turning a curve, and you will soon develop a rhythm of gently easing the fabric round as you go, continuously as you sew.

My first efforts in machine appliqué were Christmas tree place mats! They had straight boughs and branches, now I make them curved and more natural looking. They have many corners to turn, not many long edges and

Small tree for a place mat.

are ideal practice for stopping and starting, so I have no hesitation in recommending them to you to try as a beginning to machine appliqué. This Christmas tree also makes a splendid motif for a holiday calendar (add bows to hold presents, goodies, etc.) or for a baby's first Christmas quilt, especially when worked with batting in quilt-as-you-go method.

When you finish with one color thread, trim it away as close as possible to the fabric, then, when you remove the finished piece from under the presser foot, take great care not to snag the underneath loops against the underside of the foot and the feed teeth.

Turn the work over, trim away excess threads and carefully pull away the paper backing. At this stage embroider any small detail touches you may like to see on the finished result, i.e. birth dates on baby quilts, child's name, facial character lines, flower centers in forget-me-knots, etc. You can also work these by machine; with some of the most modern machines, such details can be fed into them and they will embroider automatically. Whichever method you wish to adopt, now is the time to do it.

You may alternatively decide to quilt these details into the design, either by hand, or by machine. These methods are described in the following projects.

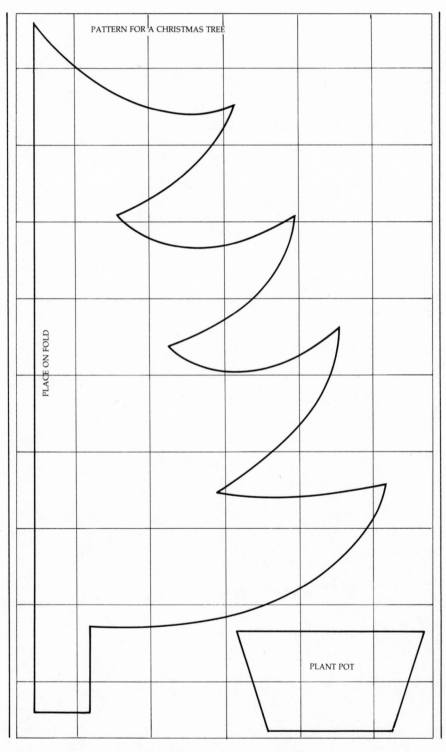

PATTERN FOR A CHRISTMAS TREE

PLACE ON FOLD

PLANT POT

Pattern for Holiday Wallhanging and Baby's First Christmas Quilt.
Method on page 64

See Plate 12 in color section

Each square = 1 inch (2.5 cm)

HAND QUILTING

INTRODUCTION

Some of the most beautiful quilts were originally made in Durham, England and are still called by this name. These have a plain top, with no appliqué or patchwork at all, and are quilted in very elaborate designs, usually centered round a medallion shape bordered with complex patterns of feathers and cables. There are many patterns available, both in paper or perforated stencils for you to work from. The peel off kind is also useful. Some of the first bed quilts came from the dockside areas when large flower sacks could be boiled and used to back old blankets. This was a poor woman's work and was sewing instead of embroidery, which was usually only taught to young ladies and practised by gentlewomen, so quilting has been slower to have its revival in the North of England. The early pioneers, the Pilgrim Fathers (or rather their mothers) took the craft to the United States, where for the last two decades it has seen tremendous popularity as a creative art form. Indeed some of the most talented quilt designers are men, probably it was the 'Fathers' after all!

This book is on the combined effects of appliqué and quilting, so I am not going into fuller details on all aspects of quilting only; there are many books and patterns about should you wish to carry this challenge further. Do try quilting only, it is a joy, and certainly one of the pleasures of life.

METHOD

REQUIREMENTS
1 2 3 4 5 6 7 8 9 10 11 14 15 17 18 19 21

When your work is completely appliquéd you will be longing to carry on and quilt it and this can be done by hand or machine. Let's start with the hand method first. There is no mystery to being able to quilt; if you can do a basic running stitch, then you can quilt. To quilt by hand for the first time is a sensation you are never likely to forget, it is very therapeutic for the mind, body and soul and is not difficult to do.

Having prepared your fabrics, right side down on to the worktable, lay a piece of backing fabric, which should be a little larger than the appliquéd block (or pieced block if you have made one from patchwork). On top of this is a piece of batting the same size, (for your first attempt I'd use 2 oz — 67 gms.) with the appliquéd block right side up on top of this. Working from the center, tack or baste outwards to the four corners then to the four sides, like the rays of the sun. Keep your small knots on top — it makes them easier to remove later on.

This is it! You are now about to take the most exciting few stitches of your life, you are starting to quilt. Thread a betweens needle 8 or 9 with quilting thread, or mercerised thread if you are being traditional. (I favor using a crewel needle which is longer and has a larger eye for threading easily.) Cut your thread approximately 36 inches (91 cms), slide it through your beeswax container and make a small knot at one end. Insert the needle approximately 1 inch (2.5 cms) away from where you wish to start quilting. This should be as near to the middle of the block as possible and with an appliquéd block it is usual to quilt round the outside of the shape as this raises it attractively.

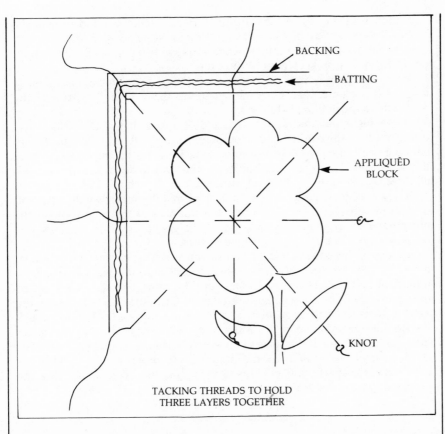

BACKING

BATTING

APPLIQUÉD
BLOCK

KNOT

TACKING THREADS TO HOLD
THREE LAYERS TOGETHER

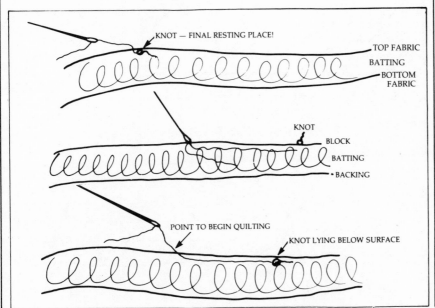

KNOT — FINAL RESTING PLACE!

TOP FABRIC

BATTING

BOTTOM
FABRIC

KNOT

BLOCK

BATTING

BACKING

POINT TO BEGIN QUILTING

KNOT LYING BELOW SURFACE

If quilted on the inside then the small hem stitches you did to hold the motif in position may pull as a result of the quilting action and won't look quite so attractive. After a little practice you may feel you would like to quilt on the inside – if so keep clear of the edge.

Back to the knot – take the needle and thread down underneath the top layer of fabric only, then raise the needle up through the top layer at the point where the quilting is to begin.

Give a slight pull and the knot should disappear below the surface and nestle neatly in the batting. Don't continue to pull, let it rest there, just before entering the top layer. Take two minute backstitches on the surface, insert the needle again as near to vertical as possible and go down straight through all three layers – the tip of the needle should just touch your finger.

By pivoting the needle on the right hand middle finger wiggle it up and down through all three layers using the thumb and the forefinger on the other hand as a pusher to make the fabric go up and down against the oncoming needle, from the opposite direction.

Try four of these to the inch (2.5 cms), you will soon become adept at how many you can manage. Ideally between six and eight is good, but it is more important that the stitches and spaces are the same size and width, rather than how many you fit in if they are uneven. Obviously you will have more stitches when the batting is thinner than when using the thicker ones. Push the needle upwards and pull through. Try not to slant the needle, as this makes the stitches and the spaces between them longer and not as neat. Aim at your stitches being all the same length as you progress, nine stitches per inch is near to perfection but this is rarely accomplished unless you are prepared to do one stitch down and one stitch up. In the Victoria and Albert

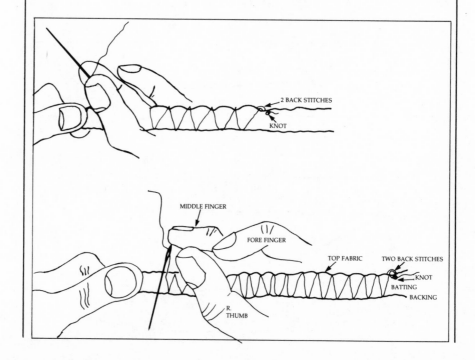

Museum in London there is a truly marvellous piece of fine quilting, a 17th century baby's bonnet, and the stitches are so small they resemble minute machine stitches.

The pivoting method, while rather unorthodox is very quick once mastered. If continuing to quilt something larger you should ideally have a floor frame which will ensure that the layers are not too taut and help you to wiggle the needle more successfully.

The above method is suitable for lap quilting or frameless quilting on your knee. Continue on around the motif, approximately $\frac{1}{4}$ inch (6mm) away from the outline. Some quilters like to leave their thread quite limp but I like to give a gentle pull to create shadows from the crimples. Whichever way you choose, be consistent and keep the tension even, or you will have a quilt that is gathered too tightly at one end and left quite slack at the other.

Depending what the subject matter is will determine how many outlines and what shape the quilting lines are. Hawaiian style appliqué is favorite with quilters as the outlines echo the design and just seem to ripple outwards towards the edge of the block. When quilting identical blocks in a full size quilt top, you will have to use a pattern and mark each block the same. However, when quilting round a scene or picture quilt, or a single cushion for example, you are freer to design your own quilting lines and make the piece individual. Following traditional patterns is a sentimental idea of recreating the past and continuing to pass on these designs for the future, but please remember the world wasn't born with a set of quilting patterns and if someone, somewhere had not 'done their own thing' they wouldn't be here today for you to copy. So please try and be original, make your piece unique and then in a century or two, who knows, someone, someday may be copying yours!

On your large frame you should try to get away from the quilt in a square only routine; when you have gained experience try an all over large quilt design.

Quilting stitches which run away from the basic shape can be used very successfully to create many interesting effects on picture quilts, i.e. two or three lines can snake across the sky from a chimney to give the impression of smoke, outlines of clouds can liven up a pale area of sky, or rays coming from the sun and undulating lines can provide waves in an otherwise uninteresting area of navy blue for the sea. Sometimes I use metallic thread for skies and seas, but it is difficult to do large areas as it always seems to break.

To trace a quilt design by the oldest method is worth a mention and may amuse you. After tracing the lines off the pattern, they were then pricked through with a drawing pin; this was easier on the end of the thumb, and the hole was larger than with a pin. Soot was then taken from the fireback and rubbed into the holes – nowadays of course, living in smokeless zones, we cannot achieve this! It is not to be recommended anyway because often the soot marks can't be washed away. A very soft lead pencil can be used through a perforated stencil and of course the controversial water erasable pen. If your home has a moist atmosphere be sure you quilt within a couple of weeks when you have marked with a pen, otherwise you may find the marks fade away and you will have to start all over again.

Something else worth a mention is a tip to stop the occasional pricked

HAWAIIAN STYLE CUSHION FABRIC REQUIREMENTS

2×16 inch squares. Plain
1×14½ inches square. Print
1×14½ inches square. Bonding agent
1×16 inches 2 ounce. Batting
1 strip 5 inches × 3 yards border print for frill
Follow the method in Project 8 for making up a cushion.

Also suitable for hand appliqué

See Plate 12 in color section

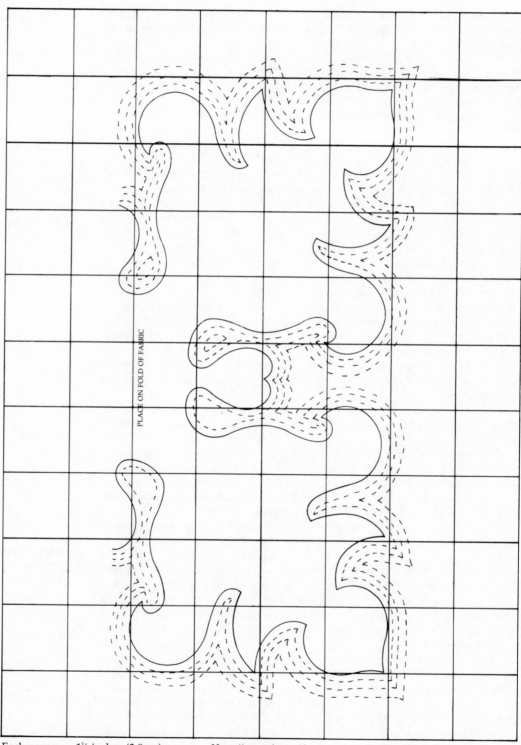

PLACE ON FOLD OF FABRIC

Each square = 1½ inches (3.9 cm)   *Hawaiian style motif*   See Plate 5 in color section

finger from bleeding and spoiling the work. Should this occur, chew a little of your thread, or moisten a piece of batting with your saliva and rub gently on the blood, it disappears like magic.

MACHINE QUILTING

METHOD

REQUIREMENTS
Pieced work, 2,   3,   4,   9,   14,   19,   20,   22

Press your pieced work.

Sandwich 4 ounce batting (135 gms.) between selected backing and the pieced top, as for hand quilting Project Three.

Thread the machine top and bottom with the same color thread, toning if possible with the section to be quilted, i.e. blue on blue sky etc.

Slide the work under the machine needle carefully so as not to catch any excess batting on the foot or needle. Set the stitch at the maximum length, and beginning as near the center as possible, sew outwards towards the edges, or round the shaped outline. You will not need to have your quilting lines set so close together as with hand quilting, never nearer than $\frac{1}{2}$ inch (1.2 cms). You may find you wish to mark the lines to be quilted, if so follow the method in the hand quilting project. Generally speaking though, machine quilting is prettier if left to follow the undulations formed by the first line of quilting stitches. Try it and you will see exactly what I mean. If you use the 'Broderie Perse' method of appliqué, (see Project Seven), you will find it easy to follow the directions shown to you by the indentations of the various designs and shapes.

See Plate 1 in color section

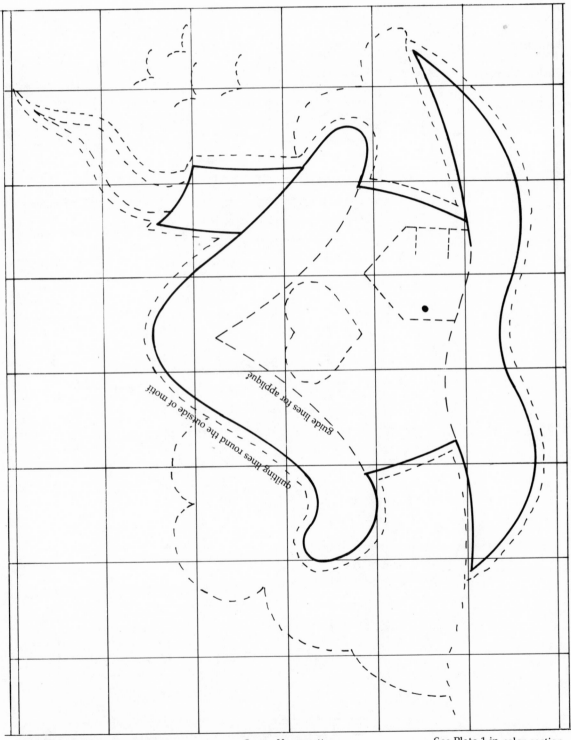

Each square = 1½ inches (3.9 cm)   *Gnome House pattern*   See Plate 1 in color section

For Hand Appliqué

When cutting out the fabric leave an extra ¼ inch (6 mm) round each pattern piece, turn under, clip into the curves, tack, pin motifs in place and hem down neatly.

Gnome House Cushion Contents

	Approx ins.	cms.	Color Key
Background	2×15×15	38×38	A
Frill	5×80	13×200	
House			
Chimney	8×6½	20.5×16	B
Window			
Door	4×1½	10.3×4	C
Grass	9×3	23×7.5	D
Roof	7×5	18×13	E
Bonding agent	10×6	25.5×15.3	

A – Lemon
B – White with small print
C – Red and Blue print
D – Green
E – Bright Yellow

Also suitable for hand quilting

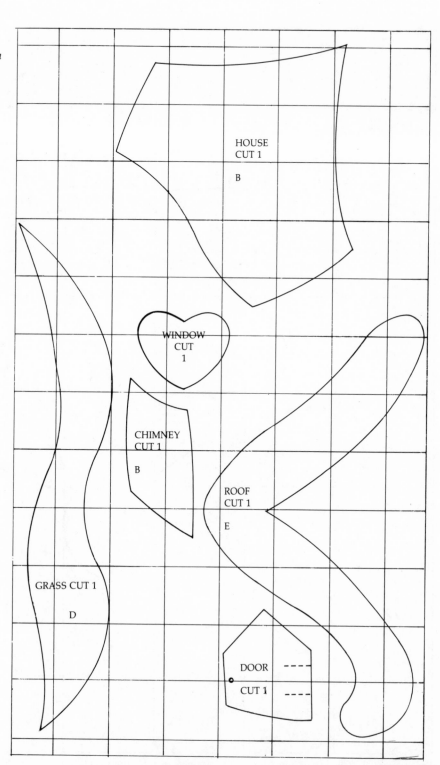

HOUSE CUT 1

B

WINDOW CUT 1

CHIMNEY CUT 1

B

ROOF CUT 1

E

GRASS CUT 1

D

DOOR CUT 1

Each square = 1½ inches (3.9 cm)

The Gnome House pattern shows the quilting lines forming smoke from the chimney, birds and clouds, also mentioned in Project 3, Hand Quilting. By joining the blocks together and frilling around the edge, this can be made into either a cushion (see Project 8) or a crib quilt.

QUILT-AS-YOU-GO

INTRODUCTION

It is quite possible to make a quilted and appliquéd project all at once that is pretty, practical and all achieved in one application. The hand enthusiasts may gasp and flinch at this point but better not to judge until tried! This method may sound quicker, though you can be assured that it is not quite so speedy and easy as it may at first appear. However, with the main requirement being yet again patience, you will soon be judging for yourself which is the correct method for you.

Using this method need only take up to nine days to design, cut and make an original king size quilt. You may think this is speedy after many weeks spent hand quilting, or it may appear slow to those of you who have come to regard machine work as a quicker imitation of 'real' quilting.

Cushion fronts can take from one hour to four hours depending on how complex the design is and how carefully you execute it and patiently perfect it.

The intricacies of 'Quilt-as-you-go' leave almost no room for error, so it will come as no surprise to you that after seven days of concentrated effort, working on a very expensive fabric, I absolutely ruined a quilt! There was no excuse, other than a second's lack of concentration, so it is better to start with a place mat and work your way up to a bedcover size.

Always give plenty of time to the design, including the careful balance of color, what goes where, and how best to quilt it.

It is not necessary to stitch through backing or lining when making picture quilts; they are not really for warmth and two layers are quite sufficient to be quilting through while appliquéing all the little cut out shapes at the same time. They can be backed once any excess batting has been trimmed away. An exception to this is with a single motif, i.e. the Hawaiian shapes which are centered on individual blocks of the usual three layers, top fabric, batting and backing, then all three layers are quilted through, attaching the motif at the same time and finally joining the squares together at the end. It is a good idea to divide the blocks with a bordered fabric and stitch down the lines printed on the cloth. You can build the largest quilts using this method; they are easier to achieve as you are not pushing masses of batting through the machine. Care has to be taken though in slip stitching the batting blocks together evenly at the edges, otherwise a 'bendy' surface will appear on a large quilt rather than a softly undulating one.

PICTURE QUILTS – HANDLING THE FABRICS

REQUIREMENTS
1   2   3   4   7   13   14   16   19   20   22

When making a picture quilt, use the batting like an artist's empty canvas and build up your work gradually on to it. Imagine the border or frame, rather than planning it; this is because the batting moves up and away, usually towards the top right hand corner. Movement usually happens where there is lots of concentrated detail in specific sections and on rather larger areas, with not so much quilting to hold it. This movement means you are constantly moving your shapes slightly and redesigning the picture a little in order to keep the overall effect balanced. Each motif should be handled differently, depending where the last one 'fell' when the machining was finished. You can use the bonding agent to keep them in place, or pin and sew them which helps the shapes retain their raised and puffy look – much prettier than a finish which is glued, and looks heavy and flat.

However, for your first attempts, if a little nervous, by all means use it, to give you confidence. Remember to keep adjusting the surface under the machine foot, easing out any puckering, backing up, or slackness, with the point of a pin, so that both surfaces lay flat together as you sew over them. As in machine appliqué, cover both fabrics evenly with the zig-zag action, making sure you don't have any raw edges peeping out. If you have the odd strand, lay the seam line tight over your finger on the left hand and trim away as close as you can to the stitches, without snagging them, using the very tip of your short, sharp scissors.

With picture quilts, you can sew across the horizon, joining land to sky first, whereas on smaller projects such as place mats or individual blocks, it is best to start stitching in the center and work outwards.

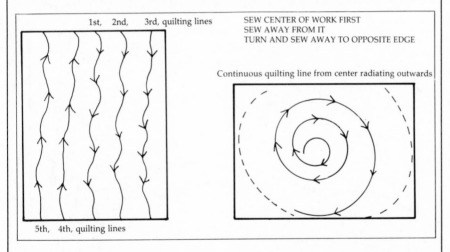

Turn the work round and stitch away from the center, this distributes the batting evenly. Build up the picture, sewing the shapes which appear farthest away from you first, and the nearest ones last of all. If using fragile fabrics for accents and highlights, i.e. gauzes, metallics, satins etc. try to stitch them on last. A good tip is to stitch them and then pin over them a spare piece of cotton fabric, so that as you are continually turning your work round, you are

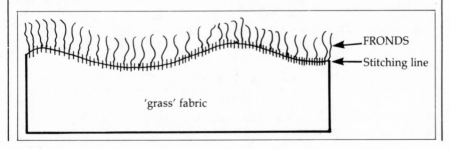

not catching the surface of these special effects, which could cause their surface to become ruffled and snagged.

Should you wish your 'grass' to have shaggy fronds, this is quite different; select the correct green, cut out the shape, leaving a small amount over on the top edge, fray this away with the point of a pin, then stitch down with the zig-zag underneath, so that the fronds look as if they are blowing in the wind!

TONAL EFFECTS WITH THREAD

If using only two fabrics for the sky and the grass (or sea) etc., give tonal effects by quilting in straight stitch machine lines, undulating along the surface, providing an interesting change of direction for the eye. The color will change automatically as the light catches it at different angles. The top thread on each set of lines can also be changed to create different effects, i.e. brown on green looks like a plowed field, yellow thread on green – a field full of buttercups, dark orange – a field at sunset, red – a field of poppies etc.

The bolder lines show only four fabrics used. The cloud, field, sun rays, bark and boughs on tree are worked with contrasting threads and machine quilting, using straight stitch.

PLACE MAT
METHOD

The method for making a sunshine place mat will be the same used for making a full size quilt.

Each square = 1 inch (2.5 cm)

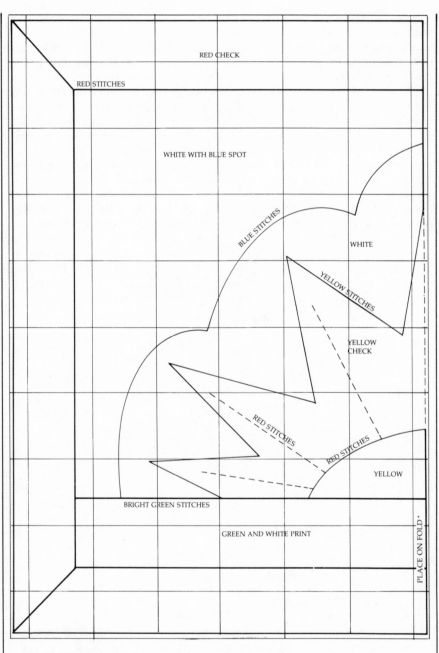

RED CHECK

RED STITCHES

WHITE WITH BLUE SPOT

BLUE STITCHES

WHITE

YELLOW STITCHES

YELLOW CHECK

RED STITCHES

RED STITCHES

YELLOW

BRIGHT GREEN STITCHES

GREEN AND WHITE PRINT

PLACE ON FOLD·

Half pattern for Sunshine Place Mat.

See Plate 12 in color section

Fabric Requirements per mat:

15 × 12 inches (38 × 30.5 cms) red small check gingham
12 × 9 inches (30.5 × 23 cms) 2 oz batting (67 grms)
12 × 1½ inches (30.5 × 3.8 cms) green and white print
12 × 6 inches (30.5 × 15 cms) pale blue spot
Small scraps white, yellow and yellow & white check bonding agent.

Trace off the sun's rays and cut out the clouds and the sun. Fold the bonding agent, tacky side together, place the cut out traced half designs against the fold and trace round each separate outline, then cut out. Open out, press down on to the reverse sides of the fabrics, and cut out following the edge of the bonding agent pattern. Peel off the paper backing.

Lay the blue spot right side up on the ironing board, place the clouds in position, center the design by the folding in half method (Project Two Diagram 9), and lining up the creases, press the clouds with a warm iron. They should now be fixed to the blue sky. Repeat with the sun's rays and finally the sun. All the bottom edges should be together in line. Lay the pressed piece on to the batting, leaving the bottom edge free and 1½ inches (3.8 cms) from lower edge of batting. Pin around the top edge, down either side and across the bottom edges. Be careful not to catch the batting under the needle or on the presser foot as you slide and turn it around. Always position your work with the bulk to the left hand side of the needle.

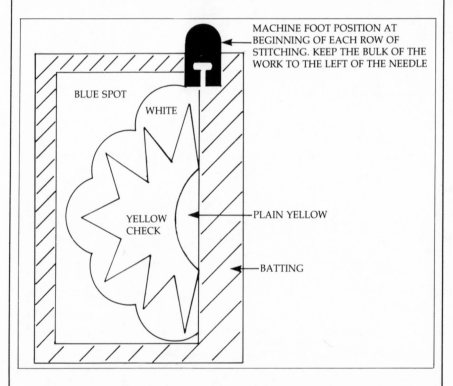

MACHINE FOOT POSITION AT BEGINNING OF EACH ROW OF STITCHING. KEEP THE BULK OF THE WORK TO THE LEFT OF THE NEEDLE

BLUE SPOT

WHITE

YELLOW CHECK

PLAIN YELLOW

BATTING

Using bright red top thread, carefully zig-zag around the curved edge of the sun, then machine outwards from the sun in imitation rays. This will push the batting outwards. With bright yellow top thread, outline the yellow check. Then with blue thread outline the clouds. Notice how using the contrasting threads makes the shapes more defined.

Trim away all excess threads and lay the green strip across the bottom edge of the appliquéd section. Notice this does not have the bonding agent on, nor do you need to press it down – this would spoil the batting underneath. Never press the fabric when it is on top of the batting, either laid on it, or when the quilt is finished, because this only causes the batting to flatten and loose its resilience. Pin, with pin heads to the left, the points to the right. This will enable you to remove them as you stitch. With a darker green top thread stitch across the horizon.

SQUARING UP AND BACKING

Using the T square, carefully check all corners are at right angles and trim away any excess batting which falls outside the measured area. Your overall work should now measure 12 × 9 inches (30.5 × 23 cms). Lay the whole section on top of the red and white check – the border should measure 1½ inches (3.8 cms) all the way round. Turn in the edges of the red check ¼ inches (6 mm) hem allowance, fold over on to the front and fix down with a pin. You will find it very easy to make sure the edges are straight, because you are using the straight lines on the checks to assist you. When reaching the corners, pinch them together, upwards, towards you. Trim off diagonally, with a little to spare, push one under the other, fold the top one down carefully and pin in place with the head of the pin to the outside corner. This is how to machine a mitred corner on the front of the work. Thread the bottom and top spools with the same color.

Commencing half way down one side, carefully zig-zag your way round the border using bright red, top and bottom, and sliding the pins out as you come to them. If there is an excess of fabric when you come to the corner, push it gently underneath the mitre before stopping the machine, leaving the needle in the work. Pivot the work and sew outwards towards the corner.

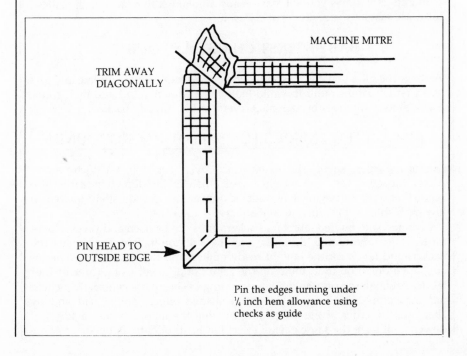

TRIM AWAY
DIAGONALLY

MACHINE MITRE

PIN HEAD TO
OUTSIDE EDGE

Pin the edges turning under
¼ inch hem allowance using
checks as guide

Trim off the threads. Insert the needle again, on the inner edge of the mitre and stitch across the next section of the border. Your borders should be flat and unpuckered with this method, while the mitres will be neat. Had you tacked the edges, it would be very difficult to get rid of any excess fabric as you move over the undulating batting. This applies with all machine quilting and appliqué, when the two methods are attempted together. The more you learn to adapt your skills by pressing down on the loose edges and using the point of a pin to ease away the fullness underneath the needle, the more you will have a wrinkle free top surface.

CHRISTMAS PLACE MATS

See Plate 12 in color section

The Christmas tree mats can be made using the same method. As a change from checks for the background you could choose an attractive Christmas print, in which case it may be advisable to turn under the hem allowance before putting the appliquéd section on top of it. Straight stitch with the machine round the edge with tiny stitches; when you come to zig-zag, these will be hidden underneath as long as you have taken care to keep them near to the turned in edge.

Tie a tiny red satin bow and stitch (by hand) to the corner of your Christmas Mat.

HOLIDAY WALLHANGING

Follow the same method using the larger Christmas tree (Project Two, page 40). This makes a perfect background for sewing bows on and by tying them with gifts or goodies you will have ready a holiday calendar, which matches the place mats, for a really festive season.

BABY'S FIRST CHRISTMAS QUILT

Without the gifts you could embroider a child's name and birthdate and give as a first Christmas quilt it would look more attractive to hand quilt round the outline of the tree through all 3 layers having already backed it.

PRE-QUILTED FABRICS FOR SPEEDY BACKGROUNDS

See Plates 9 and 10 in color section

One of the finest small crib covers I have ever seen is in the Victoria and Albert Museum and well worth a visit when in London. It is early 18th century and while having embroidered flowers, it is exquisitely quilted in tiny back stitches in $\frac{1}{4}$ inch (6mm) squares using silk.

Commercially quilted fabric for backgrounds can be used and saves a lot of time. The embroidered designs, like the crib quilt, can be traced, the background fabric can be bought ready quilted and the traced embroideries appliquéd down on to it. Build up the center of a flower using three or four fabrics sewn on top of each other, decreasing in size to the center. By picking out the colors with care, a delightful shaded effect can be had and by changing the order of the layout and rotating the fabrics round, a series of flowers will have the same overall effect but be differently applied.

Trim off the threads. Insert the needle again, on the inner edge of the mitre and stitch across the next section of the border. Your borders should be flat and unpuckered with this method, while the mitres will be neat. Had you tacked the edges, it would be very difficult to get rid of any excess fabric as you move over the undulating batting. This applies with all machine quilting and appliqué, when the two methods are attempted together. The more you learn to adapt your skills by pressing down on the loose edges and using the point of a pin to ease away the fullness underneath the needle, the more you will have a wrinkle free top surface.

CHRISTMAS PLACE MATS

See Plate 12 in color section

The Christmas tree mats can be made using the same method. As a change from checks for the background you could choose an attractive Christmas print, in which case it may be advisable to turn under the hem allowance before putting the appliquéd section on top of it. Straight stitch with the machine round the edge with tiny stitches; when you come to zig-zag, these will be hidden underneath as long as you have taken care to keep them near to the turned in edge.

   Tie a tiny red satin bow and stitch (by hand) to the corner of your Christmas Mat.

HOLIDAY WALLHANGING

Follow the same method using the larger Christmas tree (Project Two, page 40). This makes a perfect background for sewing bows on and by tying them with gifts or goodies you will have ready a holiday calendar, which matches the place mats, for a really festive season.

BABY'S FIRST CHRISTMAS QUILT

Without the gifts you could embroider a child's name and birthdate and give as a first Christmas quilt it would look more attractive to hand quilt round the outline of the tree through all 3 layers having already backed it.

PRE-QUILTED FABRICS FOR SPEEDY BACKGROUNDS

See Plates 9 and 10 in color section

One of the finest small crib covers I have ever seen is in the Victoria and Albert Museum and well worth a visit when in London. It is early 18th century and while having embroidered flowers, it is exquisitely quilted in tiny back stitches in $\frac{1}{4}$ inch (6mm) squares using silk.

   Commercially quilted fabric for backgrounds can be used and saves a lot of time. The embroidered designs, like the crib quilt, can be traced, the background fabric can be bought ready quilted and the traced embroideries appliquéd down on to it. Build up the center of a flower using three or four fabrics sewn on top of each other, decreasing in size to the center. By picking out the colors with care, a delightful shaded effect can be had and by changing the order of the layout and rotating the fabrics round, a series of flowers will have the same overall effect but be differently applied.

underneath. Never press the fabric when it is on top of the batting, either laid on it, or when the quilt is finished, because this only causes the batting to flatten and loose its resilience. Pin, with pin heads to the left, the points to the right. This will enable you to remove them as you stitch. With a darker green top thread stitch across the horizon.

SQUARING UP AND BACKING

Using the T square, carefully check all corners are at right angles and trim away any excess batting which falls outside the measured area. Your overall work should now measure 12 × 9 inches (30.5 × 23 cms). Lay the whole section on top of the red and white check – the border should measure 1½ inches (3.8 cms) all the way round. Turn in the edges of the red check ¼ inches (6 mm) hem allowance, fold over on to the front and fix down with a pin. You will find it very easy to make sure the edges are straight, because you are using the straight lines on the checks to assist you. When reaching the corners, pinch them together, upwards, towards you. Trim off diagonally, with a little to spare, push one under the other, fold the top one down carefully and pin in place with the head of the pin to the outside corner. This is how to machine a mitred corner on the front of the work. Thread the bottom and top spools with the same color.

Commencing half way down one side, carefully zig-zag your way round the border using bright red, top and bottom, and sliding the pins out as you come to them. If there is an excess of fabric when you come to the corner, push it gently underneath the mitre before stopping the machine, leaving the needle in the work. Pivot the work and sew outwards towards the corner.

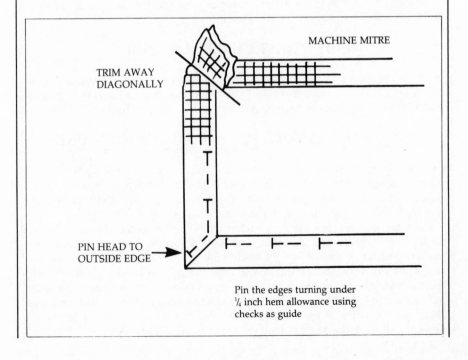

MACHINE MITRE

TRIM AWAY
DIAGONALLY

PIN HEAD TO
OUTSIDE EDGE

Pin the edges turning under
¼ inch hem allowance using
checks as guide

Plate 1   Scatter cushions — various methods from handquilting to broderie perse

Plate 2   Christmas wallhanging

Plate 3   Gingerbread men playing cricket wallhanging

Plate 4   Christmas morning wallhanging

Plate 5   Hawaiian style quilt

Plate 6   *Christmas night wallhanging*

Plate 7   *A quilt for a Silver Wedding Anniversary showing Random quilting and machine appliqué through an 8 ounce batting*

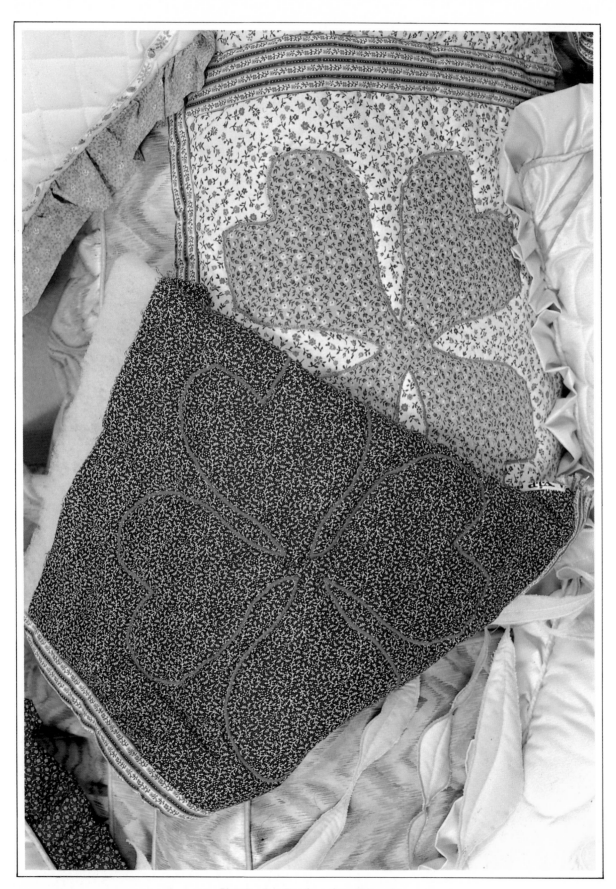

Plate 8   A section from the quilt in a day

Plate 9   *Rosette quilt*

Plate 10   *Appliquéd butterfly quilt for girl's room*

Plate 11   Frog wallhanging

Plate 12   Showing the Christmas Tree place mat, The Sunshine place mat, Hawaiian cushion, Butterfly cushion

Plate 13   Gingerbread man house wallhanging

OUTLINES

You will notice how the outlines, both in machine appliqué and quilt-as-you-go resemble the button hole stitched outlines of the arts and crafts movement appliqué work. The Glasgow School of Art founded an embroidery class in 1894, which developed an entirely new style of embroidery; many of these designs were appliquéd, using large buttonhole stitches to strongly emphasize their outlines. While these pieces were generally not quilted, it is mentioned as a guide; using heavy contrasting threads for your machine work is not an entirely new idea, but yet again another modern approach in innovative needlecraft.

LARGER PROJECTS AND PLANNING

When working on large projects it is essential to tackle your work systematically and carefully plan the overall picture design and decide exactly how you are going to quilt the work. Try and make sure that the most intricate sections of the work are positioned where it will be easiest for you to get the whole batting underneath the machine foot. There would be no point

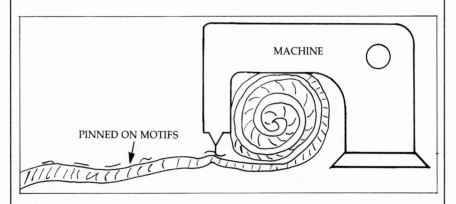

MACHINE

PINNED ON MOTIFS

in deciding to go full steam ahead with a very complicated central motif, if the king size batt will not roll and turn easily. Roll all your work, being careful with the pins, from the right, then squeeze this underneath the machine arm, sewing from the center outwards all the time; see how many lines you can stitch in one direction before turning the quilt. If you cannot quite turn a corner, it is perfectly alright to cut the thread at the end of every line. You can always machine up to it when you turn the work.

Perhaps looking at the diagrams you will see more easily how that is done, by taking as an example, the battlements of the castle on the Christmas wallhanging. Notice too how the castle is on an outside edge; don't be afraid to turn the work upside down so that you are working nearer an edge.

Planning your work also reduces neck strain; pushing against too much batting for a long, concentrated time and using the slow rhythmic swing of the zig-zag can be very fatiguing; keep pulling your shoulders back and lifting your head up. Try not to look at the needle, but keep your eyes on the front of the foot. You can't stop the needle going into the fabric after the foot,

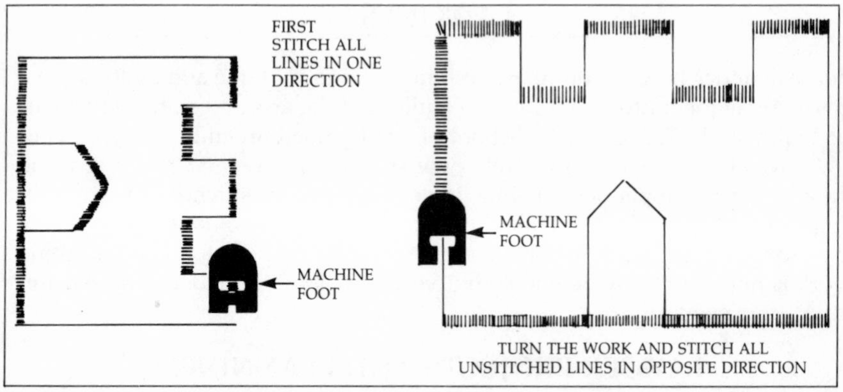

FIRST STITCH ALL LINES IN ONE DIRECTION

MACHINE FOOT

MACHINE FOOT

TURN THE WORK AND STITCH ALL UNSTITCHED LINES IN OPPOSITE DIRECTION

but you can stop going blurry eyed by watching the single, unswinging foot, and where 'it' goes the needle will follow!

LOOSE MOTIFS

INTRODUCTION

Loose motifs can give a real 3D look to your work and they are very simple to make. For example, if you random quilt a background for a cushion or a quilt it is very much easier to make small loose motifs to hand sew on to your background, than it is to actually appliqué them on as you quilt.

Flowers can look very pretty when stitched to a cardigan, and be instantly transformed into an evening jacket at very little expense. An evening dress can have loose motifs of strings of flowers, leaves and stems floating down to earth from the neck and the belt.

Loose flower motifs for quilted jacket and also on matching skirt.

See Plate 1 in color section

Use a regular dress pattern, but if you wish to quilt a bolero, don't forget that the quilting makes the fabric smaller. To overcome this, cut out from a slightly larger pattern, or better still, if using the machine do your background quilting first, before placing your pattern. Black velvet with bright colored or metallic flowers is superb, especially with sequin highlights, though don't fall into the trap of trying to make your motifs out of velvet, until you have had lots of experience. It sheds or frays badly, shows trace marks from the presser foot and slithers like a snake, so it is better to keep it for background only. Extra flowers can be used on evening bags, on shoes, dress hems and in the hair.

Children's quilts can be enhanced by loose motifs: animals which can slot into a Noah's Ark, farmyard scenes, or a Humpty Dumpty who can actually fall off a wall!

Quilted background echoing the design, the motif is attached through the center only leaving the petal tips free, also the leaves are mounted just 'kissing' the corner. The stem is appliquéd down onto the background.

See Plate 1 in color section

METHOD

REQUIREMENTS

1   2   2ounces (67 grams)   3   4   7   11   14   15   22 'Velcro' optional

If you sew a pad of 'Velcro' on the back of each caricature and a corresponding patch on the background you can swop the animals etc. around, changing the scene. Any design from a book will do to trace and cut out a pattern as you did for machine appliqué, no seam allowance needed; what you cut is what you sew. Sandwich together two layers of fabric with the batting in the middle of them. Pin the paper pattern on the top of the top layer and sew round the guide lines through the paper. Tear the paper away and there you have your outlined shapes.

Very carefully trim away the fabrics and batting with sharp pointed scissors, right up to the stitches. Take care not to snag the stitches, but likewise, don't leave any fraying ends. When you have completed this, machine round the outside edges of the shapes again, and over the first set of stitches; this gives a stronger edge and more pronounced outline.

When using flowers, you can emphasize the center with a few beads or iridescent sequins to catch the light. Black beads are useful for eyes on

Leave the sails 'free' blowing in the wind.

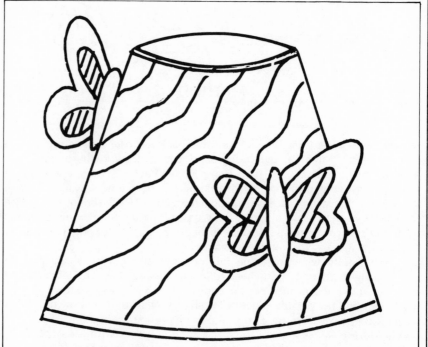

Lampshade with Butterfly wings left free —
these match the tie-backs on next page.

Curtain tie-backs using loose motifs.

animals but if giving to a child, make sure you only embroider the details on. This method can also be used to make pretty little gifts for a bazaar or party. Put dried seed heads from lavender into the batting before sandwiching into

Alternative tie-backs for Christmas.

the fabric; these will then add their perfume to a dressing table drawer. Likewise put some herbs and spices into the batting before making a tomato shaped pan holder.

Loose motifs can also be made stiffer using heavy duty interfacing for the backing layer. Large daisy shapes, hearts, bows or even the butterfly as shown on page 35 in the section on hand appliqué— these sewn on to ribbon make attractive, stiffened curtain tie-backs with a quilted look.

BRODERIE PERSE

INTRODUCTION

This is a fanciful name for the simplest of all applications — cutting out and sewing on.

How many times have you had a small length of material left when making curtains or a dress; too large to throw away, too small to make anything with and a design too large to save it for patchwork? Broderie Perse is a quick and very effective way of introducing a little color from, say, curtains, into a cushion, etc. though a little of me says it's cheating slightly, in the nicest possible way! It is also another way of being able to save a treasured remnant of designer fabric to enhance a room, which would have, in the usual way, proved too expensive to lavish around in large doses.

METHOD

REQUIREMENTS
1 (large design on remnant of curtain fabric) 4 7 14 16 20 22

Simply iron the bonding agent on to the reverse side of the part of the design you favor, peel off the paper, cut out the shape and follow the machine appliqué method, project Two. It is wise to zig-zag round the outline before appliquéing down on to the new background, as the fabric is likely to fray, especially if it is a coarse curtain cotton.

See Plate 1 in color section

If following the hand method, there is no need to use iron on backing. Cut out the design $\frac{1}{4}$ inch (6mm) larger than the actual size, turn under the $\frac{1}{4}$ inch (6mm) allowance and tack or baste the edges. Press gently, and if it is curtain cotton, use steam to give you a better crease.

Choose your background fabric with care. Glazed cotton chintz with an acrylic finish is particularly good and this prevents cracking when quilting. It also has a 'super rich' look without the impracticalities of satin. Place the motif on it, set it at an angle away from the dead center and fix in place. To do this either use the iron if using the bonding agent or pin down if hand stitching. Either way, carefully stitch round the outline, again by hand or machine. Quilt outwards from the design, as shown in the diagram.

You will now have seen the effect of using Broderie Perse. By using any method in the book you can continue to make either a cushion or quilt, by hand or machine, using larger size motifs than are usually practical for appliqué and patchwork.

MAKING UP A CUSHION

See Plate 1 in color section

METHOD

REQUIREMENTS
1   4   7   13   14   19   20

Choose and purchase a cushion pad. Unless you are allergic to them a feather pad is recommended. From the many shapes available, round, oblong, heart shaped, it is best to start with a square. Cut your backing, meaning the actual back of the cushion, ½ inch (1.3 cms) larger all round than the pad.

Take up the piece of work you have already appliquéd and quilted and trim it to the same size as the background fabric. To do this use the T square for corners, right angles and sides.

TO MAKE THE FRILL

Cut 5 inch (12.5 cms) strips from across the width of the fabric. If using a border fabric for the frilling, in which the border runs lengthways on the roll, cut the strips lengthways; the longer they are the less joins you will have. Generally speaking you will need 2½ times the outside measurement of the pad in length.

With the Imperial measurements of 45 inch wide material it was easy to say cut nine × 5 inch strips from 2½ yards in length, which will give you frilling for nine cushions, (a very useful calculation when working in a group). With metric measurements that would now be 112 cms wide material cut into nine × 12.4 cms from 2.30 metres in length.

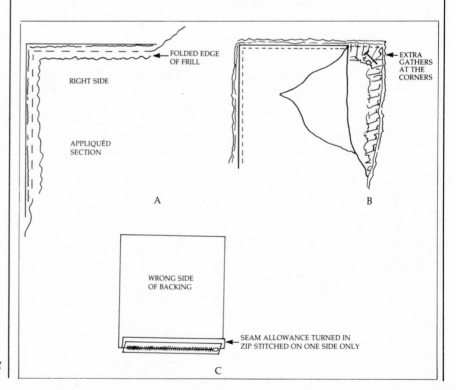

Pin down to prevent movement when sewing outside edge.

Join the edging strip on its short sides, right sides together. Press seam line open, fold in half lengthways and run a gathering thread down the raw edges which are together.

Draw this up to fit the edges of the appliquéd square. You could divide it into quarters first, marking each one with a pin, match these with the corners, then gather — this ensures even gathering. Pin all the way round the edges and then tack in place. Adjust the gathers to be fuller at the corners and pin these to the face of the work to stop them from catching as you sew.

MAKING UP

Lay the backing section on top of the frills, face down and tack round the edges again. If you would like to insert a zipper, it is necessary to sew one side of the zipper to one edge of the backing fabric, turning under a $\frac{1}{2}$ inch (1.3 cms) seam allowance as you do. Machine or hand sew round the three remaining sides, finishing off with back stitches, just round the corners on to the fourth side.

Turn right side out, unpin the corners of the frilling, turn in the fourth side and pin in the opened up zipper. If you are not practised at this then stitch the zipper by hand, with short back stitches.

When planning to make more than one cushion, think in depth. Take three colors and mix them around; what is the background for one will be the frilling for another and a motif on the third. This will stop your room looking like a mass produced market and give it a designed look.

CHRISTMAS WALLHANGING

See Plate 2 in color section

INTRODUCTION

Having worked through some of the smaller projects you are now ready to master a picture quilt. I have often been asked why this project is not in kit form or why this one can't be tackled first and can this be made from my bag of scrap materials? First, it would be impossible to put large picture quilts in kit form because the availability of fabrics constantly changes and keeping the color cö-ordination perfect would be an ongoing headache. Kits are all very well for showing you the basics, but for an adventurous composition such as this they are not practical, especially without knowing the sewing capacity of the stitcher.

The reason why it would be unwise to tackle this one as a first attempt should be obvious from all you have read previously; taking everything in stages is the quickest way to success. Lastly it is not a good idea to make this from your bag of scrap materials unless you have been collecting scraps for years with a future Christmas wallhanging in mind. The odd piece from the scrap bag is fine, but careful color co-ordination is required so as not to disturb the balance.

METHOD

REQUIREMENTS
1   2 (6 ounces, 202 grams)   3   4   7   11   13   14   15   16   19   20   22

Extras: Christmas frilled edging and Broderie Anglaise and white lace edging. Navy blue glazed chintz for the sky. Assorted Christmas prints. Some can be purchased with small toys printed on, which can be cut out and used for the presents under the tree, the soldier on guard in the sentry box, the cat by the door and the wreath on the door. Small piece of gold lamé or gold imitation leather. Organdie or voile (this can be bought with a frosted design on, but you can achieve this with small dabs of glue and some artificial snow). Satin or the reverse side of dupion for the ice effect. Any snowy type cotton fabrics -- varying shades of grey, off white, pale blue, etc.

Take time collecting together all you need for this quilt. Be like a magpie, look carefully at the fabrics chosen and understand why they are there. The small section of dark blue with stars on it, representing the milky way, was printed for the Bicentennial so it is doubtful whether you will be able to find this now, but make a near substitute with miniature polka dots on a navy blue background.

Cut out the batting, 5 inches (12.5 cms) larger than the pattern, on all sides. Trace off the shapes from the full size pattern. Make full size tracing of the pattern on a sheet of polyethylene if you can; it is better to see through as this will act as your placement guide. Decide at this stage whether you are following the pin only method, or whether you will be more confident with the bonding agent method; on such a large picture you should ideally use pin only.

Cut out the pattern pieces and pin them to the related fabrics that you have selected, and cut them out. Place the navy blue glazed chintz on first, the top edge 5 inches (12.5 cms) down from the top edge of the batting and 5 inches (12.5 cms) in from either edge. Pin round the edges carefully. Place the first two sections of hillside and then the little bit of hillside over by the castle. Pin carefully with the head of the pin to your left. Pull the bottom edges down tight and secure with pins running from bottom to top (head of the pin to the bottom). Carefully roll the bottom edge over towards the center of the quilt (the foot of the hills). Turn the roll and squeeze lengthways, right hand side first underneath the machine arm.

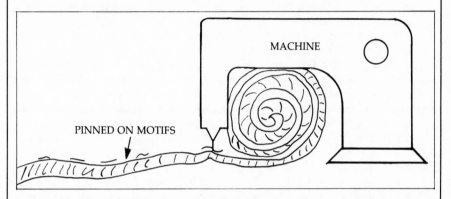

Using white thread, stitch across the horizon. If any of the edges are likely to fall behind another motif as you stitch later on, don't stitch at this stage but leave the edge free. Unroll and remove the bottom layer of pins and place the next hillside in line. Stitch across this in the same manner. Use the traced placement guide on top, sliding the pieces under to line up. The house, smoke, chimney, roof, window and door, in that order, overlapping the pieces which are nearer to you, i.e. smoke goes underneath the chimney section, which in turn lays underneath the roof edge. Keep checking to make sure stray pins are not hiding in the batting.

Turn the work upside down and work round the outlines, keeping the bulk of the batting away from you on the left hand side.

Next place the turrets (without their roofs) and the castle walls. Turn the work right way up and stitch down the turret walls, not across the top and bottom edges. Don't put the windows in at this stage. Turn the work so that almost all of it lies at the back of the machine. Just sliding the right hand edge under the machine foot, work across the walls and battlements.

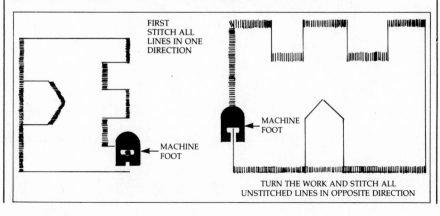

Place and stitch the sentry into his box. I imagined a cannon and outline stitched it in. Do the same for the white topped hills in front of the castle, then the hillside, with the machine-outlined path running down it.

Over to the opposite side, place the satin, or reverse side of dupion to give the shiny hillside, then the small holly bushes by the path and the bottom hills on the left hand side, then the bottom right. You will be able to manage all these last sets of hills with the majority of the appliquéd section away on your left out of the way.

Pin on the Christmas tree, then turn the work upside down and stitch bottom to top. Cut the loose threads and repeat down the other side of the tree, finishing at the top point. Stitch on the presents in the same way, slanting the work and sewing all the lines in the same direction. Slightly slant in the opposite direction and stitch the other sides of the presents. You will have now learned a lot more about batting placement under the machine foot, which will be an enormous help when tackling a larger quilt.

Stitch on the gingerbread man playing at Santa Claus then the tree on the right. Sew the little creatures, if you have them, round the cottage, with the bulk of the work on your left and the picture upside down.

Pin the starry section to the sky, then put the top edge underneath the machine with the bottom edge furthest from you, and stitch around this. Quilt outwards from it, breaking up the plain navy.

Sew the 'woodwork stripes' for the manger. Outline this carefully in dark brown. Then the roofs on the turrets in white. Continue stitching a line from them for flag poles and stitch on the triangular flags, opposite direction to the smoke if you want a deliberate mistake.

Iron a piece of bonding agent on to the back of the gold lamé pieces to stop them fraying (even if you are using the pin only method). Appliqué the three

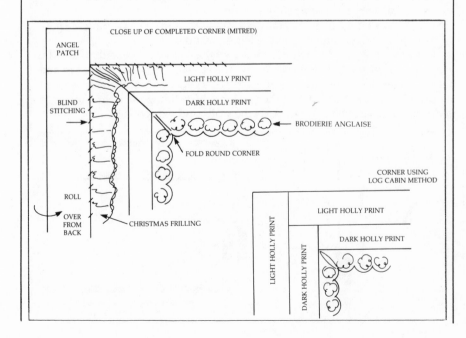

fabrics for the star together, then only appliqué and quilt them into the background, fixed together as one unit. Cover this over by pinning a piece of gauze or cotton; this will make sure it doesn't snag while you complete the gold section with the Baby in the Manger, then the windows in the turrets. When complete, cover this too. Pin and sew the lace edging to the turret roofs. Cover these while you stitch in any words that you may want. Always leave words to the end. Space them in where you think the quilt lacks quilting to break up the larger untouched surfaces. The words 'Peace, Love and Joy' in this quilt was a message to my three children, with the following meaning, Peace (underneath the house) meaning Peace in the Home, Love (by the manger) meaning love of fellow men and our religions, Joy (underneath the toy castle) meaning from the gifts we share and the pleasures of giving. When my children said it was all very well but they could hardly see the quilted words, I replied 'That is the real message and it means if you really seek hard enough in life you will find all three — 'Peace, Love and Joy' — so see if you can put hidden messages in your quilts, giving the viewer yet another puzzle to solve, after wondering how you made it from your scrap bag bits!!

Using the T square, true up the sides of the batting, and pin the Broderie Anglaise right side facing you, frilled edge inwards, around the edges of the appliquéd section. Stitch round this using white thread and a running stitch.

Cut 2 inches (5 cms) of dark Christmas print in a strip to fit around the Broderie Anglaise. Pin in place, face down, and stitch down through the sewn edge of the Broderie Anglaise using a running stitch again. Open outwards, cut a 4 inches (10 cms) strip of lighter Christmas print and lay face down on to the opened out dark strip. Pin and stitch in place with a running stitch. You may mitre the corners of these strips, or run straight off, like log cabin patchwork.

Lay the backing fabric face down on to the work table; it should be 3 inches (7.5 cms) larger than the completed work on all sides. Place the completed picture, face uppermost, pin carefully 2 inches (5 cms) in, all the way round the edge, and stitch down through all layers. At this stage you can insert a Christmas frilled edging in which case, leave the join along the bottom edge, then you can stitch a bow over the join. Fold the backing over on to the front edge and carefully blind stitch down, catching your stitches through the machine stitched line. You should now have a beautiful, rolled and padded edge to your quilt. Use this method with most appliquéd quilt edges; it's firm and attractive. To complete your Christmas picture, see if you can find some small angels in your patchwork fabric, cut them out and stitch in the corners, catch the frilled edging alongside them, they will appear to be peeping out, singing a carol perhaps?

Once you have tried one picture quilt, you can then design your own scenes – the possibilities are endless. The next project is of gingerbread men playing cricket; they could then be used in scenes playing a variety of other sports. As a complete alternative, a scene could be created of a nanny pushing a carriage; a little white frilling for her cap and dress hem.

Alternative ideas for Picture Quilted Wallhangings are Color Plates 4, 6 and 13 in the color section.

GINGERBREAD MEN WALLHANGING

See Plate 3 in color section

METHOD

REQUIREMENTS

1   2 (4 ounces, 135 grams)   4   7   11   13   14   15   16 (optional)   19   20   22

Extras: Gingham for backing
Ribbon for hanging loops

Cut out the batting 3 inches (7.5 cms) larger on all sides than the pattern. Trace off the shapes and cut out. Lay the green section across the blue, overlapping by ¼ inch (6 mm), and pin and zig-zag stitch across with a dark green thread.

Embroider any personalized details on to the door or anywhere else now if desired, or you can quilt it through later by machine. Place the clouds, sun, hills, trees and house on to the blue/green section. Pin down in that order, building the picture up as you go. Now pin round the outside edges.

Change the thread to white. Keeping the sky section to the right hand side of the needle zig-zag round the clouds.

Change the thread to red. Stitch round the house walls and sew on the 'sights board'.

Pin all the remaining shapes in place, inserting the chimney under the roof top edge, the trees overlapping the house walls etc.

Change the threads to dark green, or yellowy green for a sunny effect. When all the shapes are stitched down, you can now do the personalized details if you are machine quilting them. Machine quilt the wickets, balls and stumps in, adding small details like padding on pads etc.

Treat the background fabric in exactly the same way as the background for the place mats in Project 5. Cut it 4 inches (10 cms) larger than the batting

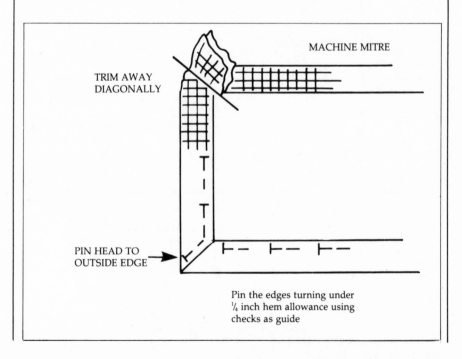

MACHINE MITRE

TRIM AWAY
DIAGONALLY

PIN HEAD TO
OUTSIDE EDGE

Pin the edges turning under
¼ inch hem allowance using
checks as guide

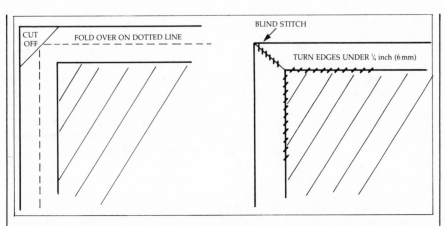

and lay the appliquéd picture face up on to it. Fold over on to front surface and turn the edges in, folding on the checked line of the gingham as a guide to keeping it straight. Mitre the corners as for machine work.

Pinning the edge in place can be quite time consuming, but this is well worth the effort; the care taken now will produce a fine finished picture-frame effect to your pieces. This type of edge can also be stitched by hand,

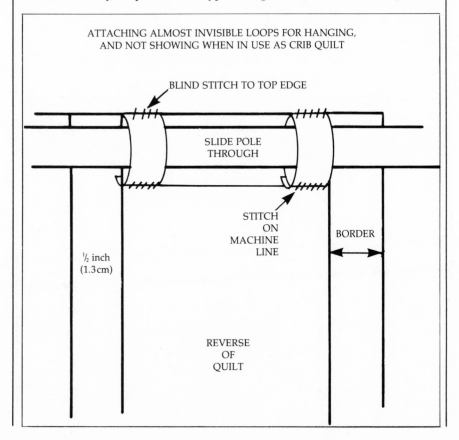

using blind hemming. If you should choose to make the quilt entirely by the hand method, however, I recommend that you work two parallel lines of quilting stitches round the edge, $\frac{1}{2}$ inch (1.3cms) apart, the first one $\frac{1}{4}$ inch (6mm) inside the turned in edge. This gives a more durable border.

A picture quilt can be used for specific purposes, other than as a wallhanging. For instance, it would make a pretty and warm cover for a baby's crib. As a wallhanging however, you will need to provide hangers at the back. These can look ugly, if visible from the front, if the quilt is in use on a crib. The best method is to attach matching ribbon loops to the gingham – cut two pieces, twice the measurement of the border plus $\frac{1}{2}$ inch (1.3cms). Fold these in half, turn the bottom edges up $\frac{1}{2}$ inch (1.3cms) and hem stitch to the backing, starting on the zig-zag line, half way between the center and the outside edge. Carry on stitching down both sides, catching the top folded edge to the top inside edge of the quilt.

Turn over, make a chunky, pert little bow from 15 inches (38cms) of the remaining ribbon and stitch this to the bottom right hand corner of the picture, adjoining the mitred corner.

FROG QUILT

QUILT WITH APPLIQUÉD CENTER

REQUIREMENTS

1   2   (6 ounces, 202 grams)   3   4   7   9   13   14   16   19   22

5   6   8   10   12   17   18   21 if making by hand.

See Plate 11 in color section

See patterns on pages 93 and 94.
White fabric – cut out 18 × 18 inches (46 × 46 cms).
Green check – cut out 2 strips 6½ × 18 inches (16.3 × 46 cms).
              2 strips 6½ × 31 inches (16.3 × 78.5 cms).
              4 leaves and reeds (diagram 1).
Green spot – cut out 2 strips 8 × 31 inches (20.5 × 78.5 cms).
              2 strips 8 × 44 inches (20.5 × 112 cms).
              4 strips 7 × 5 inches (18 × 12.5 cms).
              1 Frog Body (diagram 2).
Green, red and yellow – cut out 2 legs (diagram 3).
Red   – cut out 1 Bulrush.
Khaki Green   – cut out 1 Lily Pad.
White (small)   – cut out 2 eyes.
Black   – cut out 2 pupils.
Lemon for Backing
(sheeting can be used)   – cut out 1   square   45   ×   45   inches (115 × 115 cms).
                                4 strips 45 × 3 inches (115 × 7.5 cms).
                                6 spots for legs.

Options: Backing – if quilting by machine you may like to use a percale and cotton sheet or sheeting by the yard/metre. Velcro.

METHOD FOR HAND MAKING

When cutting out the appliqué pieces a ¼ inch (6 mm) seam allowance should be left, turned under and the pieces then hem stitched in position. Follow the method from No. 1, excluding No. 3 which is for the machine making method.

Diagram 1.

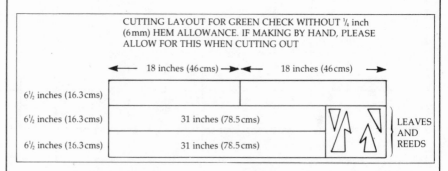

CUTTING LAYOUT FOR GREEN CHECK WITHOUT ¼ inch (6 mm) HEM ALLOWANCE. IF MAKING BY HAND, PLEASE ALLOW FOR THIS WHEN CUTTING OUT

◄—— 18 inches (46 cms) —►◄—— 18 inches (46 cms) ——►

6½ inches (16.3 cms)

6½ inches (16.3 cms)   31 inches (78.5 cms)

6½ inches (16.3 cms)   31 inches (78.5 cms)

LEAVES AND REEDS

1. Fold the white square in half and half again to find the center and center the frog's body on to it. Slide all the pieces (except eyes) underneath the body fabric using the traced placement guide for exact positioning.
2. Pin in place and tack, for hand work only.

PLACEMENT GUIDE
FOR FROG QUILT
OR CUSHION
SQUARE

Each square = 1½ inches (3.9 cm)

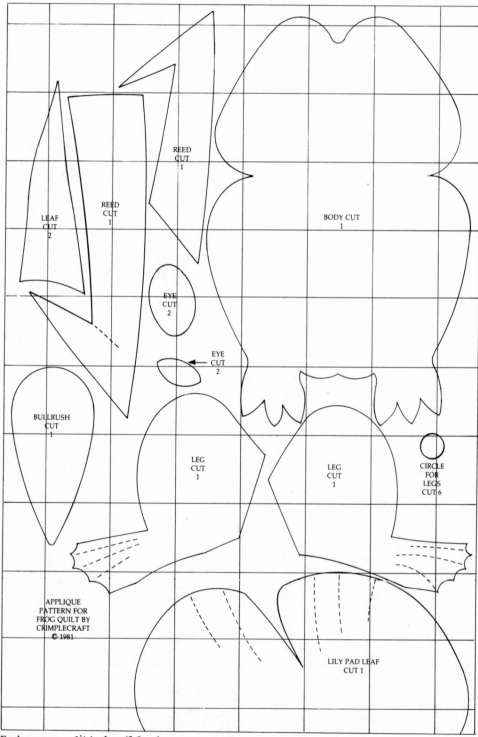

REED
CUT
1

REED
CUT
1

LEAF
CUT
2

BODY CUT
1

EYE
CUT
2

EYE
CUT
2

BULLRUSH
CUT
1

LEG
CUT
1

LEG
CUT
1

CIRCLE
FOR
LEGS
CUT 6

APPLIQUE
PATTERN FOR
FROG QUILT BY
CRIMPLECRAFT
© 1981

LILY PAD LEAF
CUT 1

Each square = 1½ inches (3.9 cm)

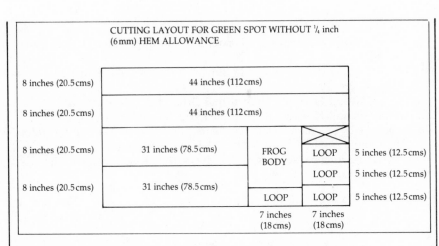

CUTTING LAYOUT FOR GREEN SPOT WITHOUT ¼ inch (6mm) HEM ALLOWANCE

8 inches (20.5cms)	44 inches (112cms)		
8 inches (20.5cms)	44 inches (112cms)		
8 inches (20.5cms)	31 inches (78.5cms)	FROG BODY	LOOP	5 inches (12.5cms)
			LOOP	5 inches (12.5cms)
8 inches (20.5cms)	31 inches (78.5cms)	LOOP	LOOP	5 inches (12.5cms)
		7 inches (18cms)	7 inches (18cms)	

Diagram 2.

For machine making

3. Using small close zig-zag stitch and a darker contrasting thread (top and bottom) stitch carefully and neatly round each piece, making sure you keep them flat.
4. Place and attach the eyes.
5. Pin the placement guide exactly over the appliquéd piece and pin at outer corners.
6. Machine through the paper, making the character lines on the frog's face, body, leaves and reeds. Then tear the paper away.
7. Trim carefully any stray threads at the back and any frayed ends on the front surface.
8. Press from the back.
9. Change to straight stitch on the machine, small running stitches by hand.

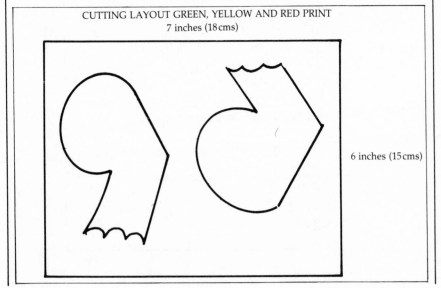

CUTTING LAYOUT GREEN, YELLOW AND RED PRINT
7 inches (18cms)

6 inches (15cms)

Diagram 3.

10. Pin the shorter lengths of green check across the top and bottom of the white appliquéd square. Stitch carefully, allowing ½ inch (1.3 cms) seam and press outwards.
11. Pin the longer lengths down the side with right sides together and stitch in place. Press outwards.
12. Repeat 10 and 11 with the green spot strips. Trim away excess.
13. Repeat 10 and 11 with lemon strips, mitre the corners if you wish.
14. Place the large lemon square on to a flat surface. Place the batting on top. Then the appliqué face upwards on top of the batting.
15. With large stitches tack through all layers from the center out to the sides and corners.

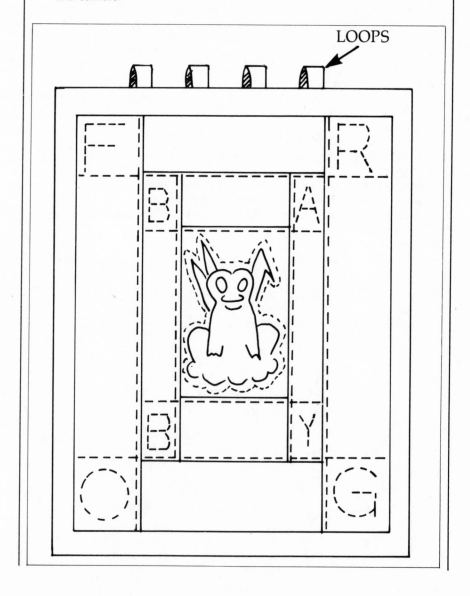

LOOPS

16. By machine or hand and using white quilting thread, outline the frog ¼ inch (6 mm) away from body and leaves, stitching through all 3 layers of fabric and batting. Outline the white square, on the seam line, where it is joined to the green.
17. Do the same round the next seam line between the two green fabrics.
18. Then again between the green and lemon.
19. Stitch the corners of each band.
20. If you feel ambitious and like quilting by hand, fill in the borders using your own quilting pattern; a letter in each corner to make a word is one possibility.
21. Turn over, trim away any excess wadding. Roll the lemon edge over the front, turn in ¼ inch (6 mm) and hem down on to the outer row of stitches, making a neat edge.
22. Stitch the four strips of green spot lengthways, turn inside out and press.
23. Fold in half and stitch 2 inches (5 cms) down on the back, top edge of the quilt at equal distances with the outside ones starting at the top of the vertical quilting lines.

The wallhanging can be hung on a pine pole or brass rod to suit your own scheme.

A small piece of 'Velcro' attached to all four corners would enable the quilt to be placed in the center of a bedspread if desired, or down quilt cover, making it detachable and reducing the need for constant washing. When necessary hand wash with care, and dry flat on a large towel. Never iron.

A 'Crimpled' effect is a quilt's nature.

This pattern can be used for scatter cushions – make the center panel up and finish off as in Project 8.

(Designed by Gail Freeman)

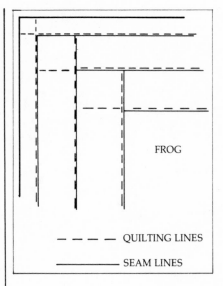

FROG

– – – – QUILTING LINES

———— SEAM LINES

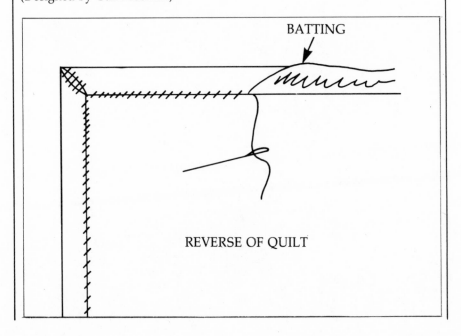

BATTING

REVERSE OF QUILT

ROSETTE QUILT

THIS IS A QUICKLY MADE QUILT FROM PRE-QUILTED FABRIC

See Plate 9 in color section

METHOD

REQUIREMENTS

1   2   (2 ounces, 67 grams)   3   4   7   13   14   19   20   22

Fabric:
Pre-quilted for background 5½ yards (4 m 90 cms).
Matching fabric for backing 5½ yards (4 m 90 cms).
Plain white – 48 × 45 inches wide (122 × 115 cms).
Blue and white pattern – 36 × 45 inches wide (91.5 × 115 cms).
Red pattern – 36 × 45 inches (91.5 × 115 cms).
Plain blue – 20 × 45 inches (51 × 115 cms).
Plain lemon – 20 × 20 inches (51 × 51 cms).

OUTER CIRCLE

Plain white – cut 4 strips 8 × 45 inches (20.5 × 115 cms), join the short ends together, press open, fold in half lengthways, and run gathering stitch down the raw edges, which are together.

   Patterned blue – cut 4 strips 6 × 45 inches (15 × 115 cms), join the short ends together, press open, fold in half lengthways, and run gathering thread stitch down the raw edges.

   Cut 76 inches (193 cms) off the pre-quilted fabric and cut to width 37 inches (94 cms). Measure from bottom edge 23 inches (58.5 cms) and mark with a

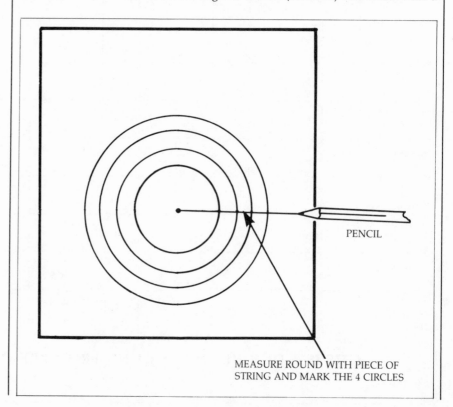

PENCIL

MEASURE ROUND WITH PIECE OF
STRING AND MARK THE 4 CIRCLES

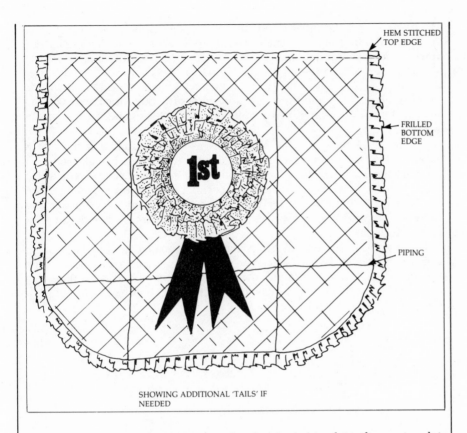

SHOWING ADDITIONAL 'TAILS' IF
NEEDED

dot. Using a tape measure or length of string pinned to the center dot, measure and draw circles on the quilted surface, first 15½ inches (16.3 cms), second 24 inches (61 cms), third 18 inches (46 cms), fourth 17 inches (43 cms).

On to the outside circle pin the drawn up gathered white frill. Stitch this in place. Straight stitch. Pin the blue pattern frill on top of it and stitch in place.

MIDDLE CIRCLE

Cut the red patterned fabric into 3 strips 12 × 45 inches (30.5 × 115 cms) and stitch and gather as before, on the next circular line. Repeat with the plain blue fabric 2 strips 10 × 45 inches (25 × 115 cms). Pin and stitch in place on the next line.

INNER CIRCLE

Cut remainder of the plain white fabric into 8 × 45 inches (20.5 × 115 cms) and repeat with the blue patterned fabric 6 × 45 inches (15 × 115 cms), pin and stitch in place on the inner line.

Cut a circle of 2 oz. batting (67 gms) 17 inches (43 cms) diameter. Cut a circle of plain lemon 18 inches (46 cms) diameter.

Run a gathering thread round the outside edge and pull up slightly. Put the batting inside it, and pat flat. Quilt '1st PRIZE' or child's name, birthdate etc. on to it, and place this section over the circle that is left in the centre of the quilt. Pin in place and stitch down; either appliqué with zig-zag, two rows – one in yellow and one in red, or blind stitch, or buttonhole stitch.

Cut the rest of the pre-quilted fabric into two 22 × 76 inches (56 × 193 cms) and one 22 × 37 inches (56 × 94 cms). Stitch the long pieces down either side of the appliquéd top and the short piece across the bottom edge. If you can manage to insert a piping then a white one would look good, as in the color photograph.

Cut the backing fabric the same sizes as the pre-quilted fabric, stitch together, lay face down on top of the quilted section and stitch all round the bottom edge. I inserted a double frill and piping in here; if you prefer a frilled edge, please follow instructions for the cushion with regard to frilling. For a boy perhaps it could be plain. For a girl, rounded corners are attractive and these are simply 2 × ¼ inch circles stitched into the corners. See diagram for complete layout.

Turn right side out, turn in the top edge and hemstitch across, this is much firmer if machined. Two tails could be stitched in place if a true rosette shape is required. Make these of fabric covered stiff material. Blind stitch the edges of the frills down to cover the raw edges and the gathering stitches of each row of frills.

A QUILT
IN A DAY

See Plate 8 in color section

INTRODUCTION

You may have often admired complicated patchwork and appliqué quilts, and even having read this book, you are probably still wondering how long they take and if only you had the time etc. Whether you are still at college, or have a full time office job with deadlines drumming in your head, or are a Mom with an endless round of washing, ironing and cooking, you may be wanting to make something, but preferably something which will be finished in a short time and before you lose the enthusiasm.

A Quilt in a Day! Impossible! But it is not! It is, however, not to be recommended for the faint of heart, the true perfectionist, or the slow of thinking!

It is quite possible though, having worked through this book, to achieve a quilt in one day. The best way to finish anything is to start first — so let's begin with the day before.

Purchase all your requirements and organize the work area. It would be no use approaching near completion, only to find that the delightful shade of hyacinth blue thread you purchased two years ago from a bargain bucket is now discontinued. You always need more thread than you think you do with machine appliqué, so buy an extra spool.

Pre-shrink all the fabrics and test for color fastness, then iron them dry.

Let's begin. Have a strong cup of coffee, a large sustaining, full of protein breakfast, or whatever motivates you to keep going without interruptions. Put more coffee on, get little Johnnie off to school, walk the dog, take the 'phone off the hook, lock the door, order a take-out if 'they' are all expecting a hot meal when you are exhausted and trying like mad to make your final stitches as neat as the first. Put up the ironing table, if you didn't do it yesterday.

METHOD

REQUIREMENTS
1   2   (4 ounces 135 grams)   3   4   7   11   13   14   15   16   19   20   22

Yard stick, cutting board and a rotary cutter would speed up the cutting of the strips.
Fabric sizes for finished quilt size approx. 48 × 62 inches.
Batting – 48 × 62 inches (122 × 157.5 cms).
Backing – 45 × 60 inches (115 × 152.5 cms).
Background – 45 × 60 inches (115 × 152.5 cms).
Motifs – 33 × 44 inches (84 × 112 cms).
Border in strips lengthways 44 × 70 inches (112 × 175 cms).

Remember this is a quick quilt for the top of a single bed. If you wish it to hang down the sides or cover the pillows then another set of blocks should be added on the top and one side.

CUTTING OUT

Cut the batting into twelve 16 inch (40.5 cms) squares.
Cut the backing into twelve 15 inch (38 cms) squares.
Cut the background fabric into twelve 15 inch (38 cms) squares. If the

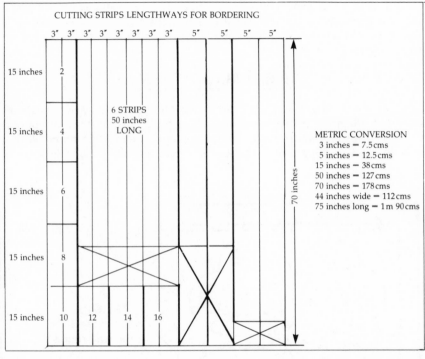

CUTTING STRIPS LENGTHWAYS FOR BORDERING

6 STRIPS
50 inches
LONG

METRIC CONVERSION
3 inches = 7.5 cms
5 inches = 12.5 cms
15 inches = 38 cms
50 inches = 127 cms
70 inches = 178 cms
44 inches wide = 112 cms
75 inches long = 1 m 90 cms

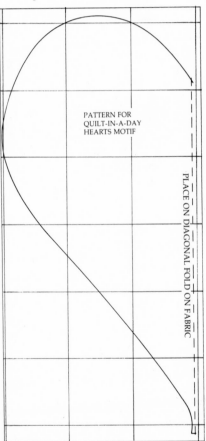

Each square = 1 inch (2.5 cm)

PATTERN FOR
QUILT-IN-A-DAY
HEARTS MOTIF

PLACE ON DIAGONAL FOLD ON FABRIC

cotton is of very good quality, then the quickest way is to tear all of these (not the batting).

Iron the bonding agent on to the back of the fabric you are using for the appliqué. Peel off the backing paper. Cut the appliqué fabric into twelve 11 inch (28 cms) squares. Fold each in half and in half again, then in half on the diagonal to form a triangle. Pin the open edges together.

Cut out the heart shape appliqué pattern and pin, in turn, on to the folded and pinned appliqué fabric. Cut out each heart (12). Even though you are working at speed, take care cutting out, what you cut is what you sew.

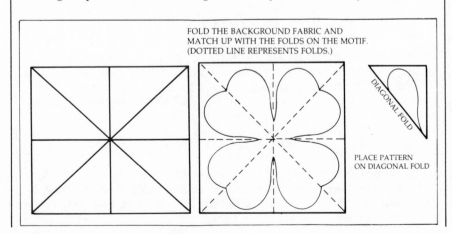

FOLD THE BACKGROUND FABRIC AND
MATCH UP WITH THE FOLDS ON THE MOTIF.
(DOTTED LINE REPRESENTS FOLDS.)

DIAGONAL FOLD

PLACE PATTERN
ON DIAGONAL FOLD

Fold each of the background squares in half and in half again, then press with the iron. Matching the folds with folds on the hearts, place each heart in the center of each square. Press down with a warm iron. They will now be fixed in place.

PREPARING TO SEW

Lay a square of background fabric face down. On top of this place a square of batting overlapping the background by ½ inch (1.3 cms) all the way round. On top of this face up, place the ironed appliqué squares. Pin round all the outside edges, making sure the batting is evenly showing on all sides.

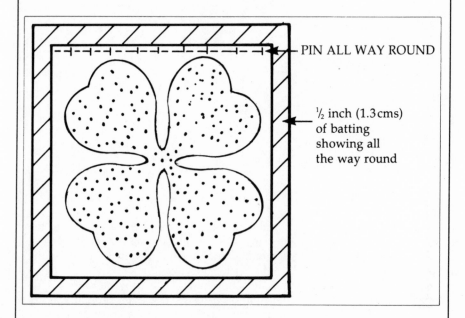

PIN ALL WAY ROUND

½ inch (1.3 cms) of batting showing all the way round

SEWING THE SQUARES (BLOCKS)

Set the machine at a close zig-zag stitch, use a contrasting thread to the backing fabric underneath and a contrasting thread to the heart shape on the top. Start in the center of each block and stitch round all twelve heart motifs, one square at a time – you may be working quickly but you can't sew twelve at once!

BORDER CUTTING

Cut the striped or border printed fabric into eight 3 inch (7.5 cms), four 5 inch (12.5 cms) strips lengthways, following the cutting guide again. You may be able to tear this, though you may save time later on by cutting now, as the torn edges ravel easily and get in your way.

BORDER SEWN ON REVERSE SIDE

BORDER STRIPS STITCHED TO ONE SIDE OF 8 BLOCKS
TURN BLOCKS OVER AND SEW 8 MORE STRIPS DOWN THE SAME
SEAM LINE

SEWING BORDERS TO BLOCKS

Cut eight 15 inch (38 cms) from the 3 inch (7.5 cms) strips. Pin these down the right hand side of eight of the blocks, with the right sides of the fabric facing one another, the pin line should be $\frac{1}{2}$ inch (1.3 cms) in from the edge of the fabric. Push the pins through all the layers. Stitch in place using a long straight stitch.

Cut another eight 15 inch (38 cms) from the 3 inches (7.5 cms).

BACK OF BLOCKS

Turn the sections over, sew 8 more strips down the same seam line allowances as you go.

If you need a break take it now and have lunch!

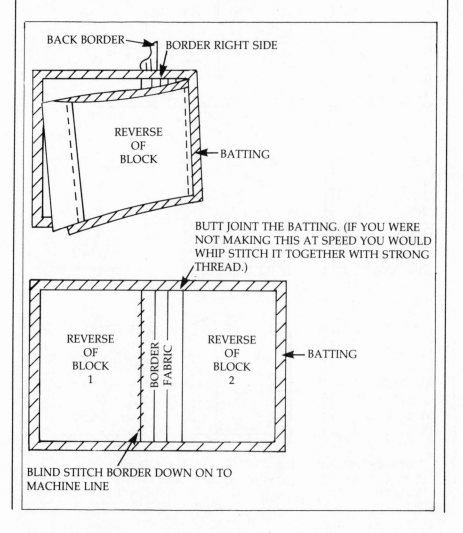

BACK BORDER — BORDER RIGHT SIDE

REVERSE
OF
BLOCK

← BATTING

BUTT JOINT THE BATTING. (IF YOU WERE NOT MAKING THIS AT SPEED YOU WOULD WHIP STITCH IT TOGETHER WITH STRONG THREAD.)

REVERSE
OF
BLOCK
1

BORDER FABRIC

REVERSE
OF
BLOCK
2

← BATTING

BLIND STITCH BORDER DOWN ON TO MACHINE LINE

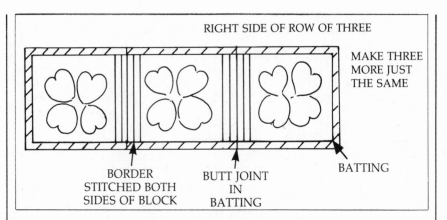

RIGHT SIDE OF ROW OF THREE

MAKE THREE
MORE JUST
THE SAME

BATTING

BORDER
STITCHED BOTH
SIDES OF BLOCK

BUTT JOINT
IN
BATTING

BLOCKS INTO ROWS

Take two blocks, with strips down right hand edges, right sides facing, and place the free edge of the front border down the unbordered side of the other block. Pin ½ inch (1.3 cms) in from the edge of the fabric, and machine down with straight stitch. Repeat this with the third block, which hasn't a border on either edge.

Make three more rows like this. Turn over and slip stitch the back borders down over the batting, turning in ½ inch (1.3 cms) as you go.

JOINING THE ROWS TOGETHER – FRONT

You will now have four rows of three blocks with borders in the center.

Using the remaining 3 inch (7.5 cms) border fabric, cut 6 strips 50 × 3 inches (127 × 7.5 cms), lay the long lengths across one front edge of one row, and pin carefully keeping the ½ inch (1.3 cms) seam allowance as before, with the border face down on to the front of the block. Machine straight stitch across.

Open out and lay the next set of three face down on to it. Pin across, checking that you are lining up the blocks with their opposites which have just been sewn. Stitch across and repeat with the third row.

Turn the quilt over and do the same on the back, blind stitching by hand to the machine stitched lines.

EDGES

Cut two 50 × 5 inch (127 × 12.5 cms), and two 70 5 inch (178 × 12.5 cms). Pin and stitch across the top and bottom edges, on the front side, face down. Turn them over towards the back, pin in place, turning under a ½ inch (1.3 cms) seam allowance as you go. Blind stitch this to the machine stitch line, turn in the corners and repeat with the longer strips down either side.

Congratulations — you have now completed an appliquéd and quilted quilt in one day and there is still time to put your feet up and admire it before everyone else does!

Put your initials, or your full name in the corner, why not? Be proud of your

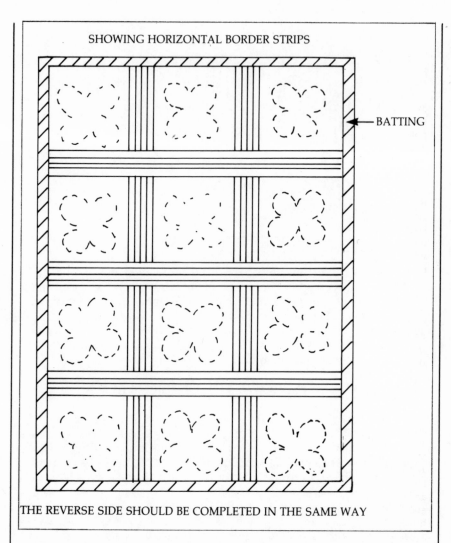

SHOWING HORIZONTAL BORDER STRIPS

— BATTING

THE REVERSE SIDE SHOULD BE COMPLETED IN THE SAME WAY

work, even if it is a speedy one – you at least have the satisfaction of knowing you have achieved it in one day, so put the date on as well, just to remind you in the future.

★   ★   ★   ★   ★

I hope you have enjoyed the various ways of approaching quilted appliqué and will try them all, choosing your favorite method. You can then carry on designing and creating many more pretty and practical projects. Thank you for buying and reading my book, it has given me a great deal of pleasure working through my craft with you. Hopefully you will now have as much pleasure in sharing your touchable, loving quilts, with friends and relations for generations to come. I'll leave you with this thought, 'Just like friends – there is no quilt like an old quilt' – so make one today, then it will be older quicker – and you'll love it for longer!

INDEX